Political Science and Political Knowledge

By Philip H. Melanson

FOREWORD BY MAX LERNER

Public Affairs Press, Washington, D. C.

To Judith

FOREWORD

"The tree of liberty," wrote Thomas Jefferson, "must be refreshed from time to time with the blood of patriots and tyrants." In a similar vein one might add that the tree of social theory —including, of course, political science—is refreshed by the sweat and blood of theorists willing to do the hard, largely thankless work of close thinking about valid and fruitful methods of social reasoning. Philip Melanson's book, packed with tight analysis, takes its place as a valuable part of this age-old, endless re-thinking and renewal.

Without saddling the author with my views, I may be permitted some reflections of my own which his book has set in motion. There are three principal, linked problems that are involved, with which all of us must wrestle: the role of intellectuals, and specifically political scientists, as a professional elite in the new knowledge society; their relation to the power structures and interest groups; and the questions of professional ethics and personal integrity that they encounter—questions that involve both the misery and grandeur of the political thinker's vocation.

The author explores each of these areas and their complex relationships with fruitful results. He drives a wedge of direction through the mass of recent literature, emphasizing some of his imperatives: the need for a sharper use of the "sociology of knowledge," applying it to political knowledge; the futility both of fuzzy "grand theory" and of piled-up empirical research and "vocational knowledge" which has no underlying self-critical philosophy of method; the treacherous pitfalls of some of the currently fashionable schools of political study, especially of the "behavioral" school and of the whole thrust toward a logical positivism; the need for more rigorous "epistemic canons" of political reasoning as a foundation for valid knowledge; the seductions of the *eidola* (in Francis Bacon's sense) of both the power groups and the powerless groups in the society and of the prestige groups of the profession; the danger of the too easy assumption that a solution of the problems of epistemology (reasoning toward a hard "science") will also bring about a solution of the problems of professional ethics (involvement or non-involvement with governmental power and with political "causes"); above all, despite his scepticisms, the author's underlying belief that the problems of political knowledge and political science can yield to a more conscious and scrupulous sense of professional responsibility.

Melanson's wide-ranging forays sent this reader, for one, back to several of the earlier efforts to map out an attack on some of these problems, by scholars in their own day. Max Weber, lecturing and writing in a pre-Hitler Germany already torn between rationalism and irrationalism, and absorbed with every vocation and every ethic, was bound to shed light both on the vocation and ethic of social theory. Karl Mannheim and Karl Popper, both of them pillars of the sociology of knowledge, each in different ways carried on a dialogue with Marxist theory—Mannheim's focusing on his twin concepts of "ideology" and "utopia," Popper's on his attack on "historicism" and his concept of the "open society" and what it implies for creative thinking.

In America the critical questions have been raised by the broader social theorists rather than the political scientists. Thus Robert Lynd's "knowledge for what?" (his answer: for changing the society); thus the stress of C. Wright Mills on playing a dissenting role in the society through the "sociological imagination"; thus the work of W. I. Thomas on "defining the situation'," of Florian Znaniecki on the sociology of "men of knowledge," of Robert Merton on the sociology of science; thus the pathbreaking work of Thomas Kuhn on the history of scientific revolutions, seen in terms of successive views of the cosmos which become models ("paradigms").

In American political science, which has largely escaped the influences from sociology, the general direction has been deflationist and reductionist—to move away from the high-flown and eliminate what cannot be reduced to provable propositions and the methods of science. Perhaps the strongest thrust has been in the "behavioral" direction, with roots going back to logical positivism in philosophy and to behaviorism in psychology. At its strongest this strain is crossed with the logical deductive method in the work of men like David Easton and Robert Dahl, and with the methods of psychiatry and psycho-history in Harold

Lasswell's work on political personality and on the "policy sciences." But more often I have encountered it in the naive form of asserting that it isn't true political science unless it is reduced to behavior that can be observed, measured, counted, fed into a computer, and given "policy" application.

The author has cast his net widely among these thinkers and others, has read prodigally in them, and—more important—has passed them through the prism of his own thinking, which is almost always different from theirs. He doesn't treat them tenderly. He is democratic in administering rebukes to writers who—he feels—have misled the profession, without regard to their age, sex, political persuasion, professional prestige, or country of origin. There is a dry but biting Veblenian irony which rubs some clinical salt into the wounds he deals out. I must confess that this has added to the delight of the book for me, since I have as much of a sadistic streak in me as the next person. I should add that at times I have somewhat ruefully recognized some of my own vulnerabilities which I have shared with a few of his targets.

The thinking is severe and packed, the style is difficult, and at times more jargon creeps into it than I might have wished to see there. But this is more than counterbalanced by the richness of resonance that the author's thinking carries with it. These are not bloodless battles of the categories in an anemic academic setting. The author has thrust himself into a life-and-death struggle to clarify our assumptions, examine the dryness of our powder, clear away whatever clogs and confuses our political thinking. What I like best about him is his recognition of the polar opposites and paradoxes in the bare frame of valid thinking, which transcend the traditional angles of vision—liberal conservative, radical—and make them largely irrelevant.

I don't say that the anguished concern about methods of thinking will itself produce great political thinkers again, after a time that has been so barren of them. The giants, with a creative life-force in them that defies analysis, usually break all the rules when they come. But we have a better chance of making our ground fertile for them if we can clear it of the weeds and undergrowth that infest it today.

MAX LERNER

New York City

ACKNOWLEDGMENTS

I am very grateful to those who in various ways have helped me to undertake and complete this book. Edgar Litt, University of Connecticut, provided intellectual encouragement and insight that was an invaluable stimulus to this work. G. Lowell Field, also of the University of Connecticut, has been a source of unique perspectives on politics and on the profession. Lauriston R. King, now a special assistant for marine affairs with the National Science Foundation, gave generously of his time and energy in serving as critic and intellectual clinician.

Helpful comments and criticisms on portions of the manuscript were rendered by Paul F. Kress, University of North Carolina, and George F. Cole, I. Ridgeway Davis, W. Wayne Shannon, and Kevin R. Guernier, all of the University of Connecticut; and by my colleague Jack W. Fyock, of Southeastern Massachusetts University. Mrs. Betty Seaver deserves much thanks for her excellent typing and editing of both the preliminary and final drafts.

It is with special gratitude that I acknowledge the continuous and energetic help of my wife Judith, to whom this work is dedicated, who not only typed and edited earlier drafts from nearly incomprehensible scribblings, but patiently listened to hours and hours of monologues about the substance, progress, and goals of the work.

PHILIP H. MELANSON

Southeastern Massachusetts University
North Dartmouth, Massachusetts

CONTENTS

"There is no way in which any social scientist can avoid assuming choices of value and implying them in his work as a whole. Problems, like issues and troubles, concern threats to expected values, and cannot be clearly formulated without acknowledgment of those values. Increasingly, research is used, and social scientists are used, for bureaucratic and ideological purposes. This being so, as individuals and as professionals, students of man and society face such questions as: whether they are aware of the uses and values of their work, whether these may be subject to their own control, whether they want to seek to control them."—C. Wright Mills, *The Sociological Imagination,* 1959.

I

Introduction

Since the time of Plato and Aristotle men have devoted their intellectual energies to the study of political life. They have usually done so not as detached, casual observers, but as impassioned advocates, for it has long been realized that how men can and do govern themselves is of paramount importance to the problems and opportunities of human existence. Because politics has historically been viewed as a crucial arena for solving the classic problems of ethics, metaphysics, and the human condition, man has not been content to argue and specluate about the realities and potentials of political life, but has sought to "know" its problems and pitfalls.

The goal of a science of politics has had a long and uneven evolution from Plato to the behavioral approach. Whatever forms in which it was manifested, whoever pursued it, whatever its successes or failures, the goal was to "know" validly answers to certain questions. More so than in any previous historical era, there exists a baffling array of observations, data, arguments, and hypotheses. This multiplicity of sources is very often labeled and employed as political "knowledge." While a Platonic guardian class has not materialized in American society, there is a highly trained and specialized scholarly community whose delegated intellectual and occupational responsibility is that of producing, certifying, and working with such "knowledge." This community is largely synonymous with the academic profession of political science.

This book examines political knowledge and the intellectual milieu of its producers from a perspective that has been severely neglected in the past. The major concern here is not with assessing the biases, injustices, or beneficence of this knowledge vis-à-vis American politics and society, nor with its impact upon the vitality or extension of democratic values, but with the goal of a

1

science of politics and with the degree and manner of its realization. The emphasis is upon conditions internal and external to political science that shape its pursuit of scientific knowledge.

Consideration will be given to salient characteristics of American society, for its complexity, interdependence, technological advancement, and political conflicts provide an important context for intellectual endeavor. More specifically, the demands for and uses of various kinds of "knowledge" and "expertise" by policy makers (especially at the federal level) constitute a key dimension of any public policy role. The goals of, and pressures upon, these primary "consumers" of knowledge are a crucial influence in shaping the consequences of research.

The occupational milieu of the major producers and purveyors of political knowledge, academic political scientists, is another analytical focus. The discipline is examined not only as an intellectual endeavor, but as an organized, academic profession with its own norms, career patterns, modes of training and socialization, and reward system. Professional structure and processes are exceedingly important in determining how and why the goal of a scientific knowledge of politics is pursued. The very definitions of "science" and "knowledge" are, to a significant degree, spawned by professional dynamics. These factors shape both the study of political life and the lives of those who study it.

Last, and perhaps most important, is an examination of the "knowledge" itself. A major assumption here is that there are different kinds of knowledge possessing different capacities, limitations, and epistemological derivations. Another is that perceptions and misperceptions of these differences by the producers and consumers are crucial to both the attainment of science and the outcomes of public policy involvement. The underlying question is: "How do we know what we claim to know?" Definitions of "science" and "knowledge" and criteria for discerning their presence or absence are, in the age of "big science" in America, the predominant way of answering this momentous question.

In contemporary political science, "how we know what we

claim to know" is structured by the interactions of cultural and historical foundations of the American political system, internal processes of academic professionalism, and methodologies and epistemologies employed in the conduct of inquiry. These elements combine to form a web of influence affecting both the values that research serves or neglects and its political uses, beyond the ideology or intent of scholars. These dynamics will be a primary focus of succeeding chapters.

What follows does not pretend to constitute an overarching critique of power and politics in America. Nor is the analysis uninformed by or isolated from the injustices, policy crises, and moral dilemmas of the political system. These are relevant to the conduct of inquiry and are included as they relate to the professional, ideological, and intellectual orientations of political scientists. They do not, however, provide either the basic motivation or the perspective for analysis. Many of the more standard critiques of knowledge, political power, and the profession's public policy role have been purposely excluded as major thrusts of analysis. This is not to denigrate their importance, but is done because this analysis seeks to transcend the behavioralist, anti-behavioralist and fact-value debates that have previously tended to dominate introspective efforts. In contrast, it assumes a perspective self-consciously divergent from many standard professional dialogues concerning political knowledge, and in so doing defines the problems in different ways that suggest different "solutions"—if any solutions do, in fact, exist.

Political science has become increasingly introspective about its collective existence as an academic profession and about its role in American politics. The stimuli provided by the policy crises and political issues centering around conflict in Indochina and the problems of race and ecology have generated a new intensity of concern and scope of awareness. For example, the implicit ideological biases of much behavioral scholarship have been illuminated. Patterns of service and "relevance" vis-à-vis various publics and institutions have been discerned and debated.

While advocates of a reorientation of professional patterns and values abound, the profession knows too little about the conditions that actually shape its public policy role, especially about the nature of its "knowledge." Too often, critics condemn the profession without providing any meaningful analysis of the conditions and dynamics that shape what it does and does not do.

The profession has recently become more cognizant of some of the relationships between its knowledge and public policy mostly because many political scientists oppose the values that they perceive as being sustained by such relationships. Political science is aware that policy makers listen selectively to the counsel of its scholars. It is aware that the "knowledge market" and the "multiversity" have drawn its "expertise" into what many view as an unsavory complicity with government, epitomized by the bizarre and abortive "Project Camelot," or perhaps by the policy exploits of Henry Kissinger. Many within the profession are concerned about what they perceive to be its neglect of deprived publics: the Blacks, the poor, and alienated youth. Such criticisms are useful and even necessary, but they do not constitute an adequately informed professional-intellectual consciousness. Nor can moral indignation or exhortations for a more "relevant" posture toward contemporary problems by themselves provide a knowledgeable basis for any value reorientation of the profession.

To advocate drastic professional reorientation without effectively analyzing how and why existing patterns and consequences emerged is more cathartic than effective. The roots of the present state of political knowledge and of its policy impact are too deep, and the causes too complex, to allow for instant alteration through political evangelism or ideological confrontation. Instead, political science must scrutinize its societal context, its professional structure, process, and culture, and its epistemological commitments—these in large measure determine *which* values the profession can and does serve.

II

Political Knowledge
in the Knowledgeable Society

American political science, like all professions, is to an important degree a creature of the society in which it exists. The complexity, technological advancement, political experience, and cultural foundations of American society necessarily help to shape the profession's intellectual and occupational configuration. This chapter deals with several prominent influences that contribute to the broad milieu of political inquiry.

Perhaps the most salient of these influences is the way in which society perceives "knowledge" in general. Broad cultural perspectives on knowledge, and on its development and uses, are bound to influence the pursuit of a given kind of specialized knowledge. Robert E. Lane has described America's orientation in this regard through the concept of the "knowledgeable society" in which "there is much knowledge, and where many people go about the business of knowing in a proper fashion. As a first approximation to a definition, the knowledgeable society is one in which, more than in other societies, its members: (a) inquire into the basis of their beliefs about man, nature, and society; (b) are guided (perhaps unconsciously) by objective standards of veridical truth, and, at the upper levels of education, follow scientific rules of evidence and inference in inquiry; (c) devote considerable resources to this inquiry and thus have a large store of knowledge; (d) collect, organize, and interpret their knowledge in a constant effort to extract further meaning from it for the purposes at hand; (e) employ this knowledge to illuminate (and perhaps modify) their values and goals as well as to advance them." [1]

Lane asserts that just as "the affluent society" has its foundation in economics, the knowledgeable society has its roots in epistemology and the logic of inquiry. Its commitments to the production and application of knowledge and to the meliorative potentials of reason pervade its culture and processes.

But the cultural foundation of the knowledgeable society in America precedes even the technological revolution that brought it to fruition. The Enlightenment faith in man's ultimate rationality and perfectibility and Classical Liberalism's faith in the judgment of an informed citizenry are very much the philosophical precursors of the orientations which Lane describes. In the emerging culture that Alexis de Tocqueville depicted, the absence of rigid class distinctions, the severing of traditional communities, and the glorification of individualism and egalitarianism led to an exceedingly fluid psychological existence that nurtured what Lane terms the "thoughtways of the knowledgeable society." [2]

In traditional, aristocratic societies, the opinions of those holding arbitrary power over life, death, and well-being were the most relevant kind of "knowledge" for the common man, regardless of their empirical or logical validity. This situation contrasted sharply with the psychological orientations in the new American democracy that derived from the emphasis upon achievement, mobility, and self-reliance. The political and psychological ramifications of egalitarianism contributed to the development of the characteristic "thoughtways."

Though the "liberal" values and ideals associated with the inception of our political system were conducive to the evolution of the knowledgeable society through the erosion of traditional patterns of power and privilege, it was subsequent historical experience that firmly implanted the foundation. America's rise to unparalleled material success, which dwarfed previous notions of human progress, was telescoped into less than two centuries of whirlwind development from agrarianism to abundance. Applied knowledge came to be perceived as the crucial link between freedom and abundance.[3] Knowledge came to be viewed as a natural outgrowth of commitments to political freedom and educational enlightenment (which in turn were perceived as intimately, if not causally, related). Abundance was not attributed solely to geopolitical determination, manifest destiny, or divine will, but also to the freedom to pursue knowledge and the incentives to apply it provided in a democracy.

The coincidence of expanding enlightenment and material progress was a potent influence on the perspectives of the producers, guardians, and apostles of knowledge: the intellectuals. The American intellectual tradition evidences a strong penchant for notions of progress and Utopia.[4] It has an underlying faith in the ultimate perfectibility of mankind and in the ultimate beneficence of knowledge.[5] Its reverence for the meliorism attending the application of human intellect to human ecology has evolved toward a cultural glorification of "knowledge" and "science" that often approximates a secular religion.[6] This view came to have both mass and elite manifestations.

Mass attitudes toward knowledge, rooted in democratic political culture, and the traditional perspectives of America's intellectual elites have a common ground in an historical experience of progress and abundance, and have been reinforced by it. The convergence of of egalitarianism, the progressivism and utopianism of the American intellectual tradition, and the world's most widely distributed material prosperity has blurred cultural perceptions of the uses and roles of "knowledge."[7] Our society tends to glorify this commodity and to grant much deference, sometimes uncritically, to anything that may be perceived to constitute it. In general, the beneficence of most knowledge is assumed. These developments and perceptions not only helped to foster the orientations observed by Lane, but intimately bound them to political culture.

Once established, the knowledgeable society possesses a cumulative, self-sustaining drive toward the production of new knowledge and new applications of old knowledge. The sheer amount and sophistication of America's knowledge and technology assure that the traits of such a society will be perpetuated and intensified, for the immense complexity and interdependence of the American technocracy render them an organic facet of evolution. The exigencies of technological development coupled with America's reverence for enlightenment tend to make the role of "knowledge" appear constant and natural, and this in turn obscures the novelty of the knowledgeable society and many of its implications and consequences.

In contemporary America knowledge is increasingly "scientific" and increasingly synonymous with "science."[8] Spencer Klaw has labeled scientists "the new Brahmins" in order "to convey a sense of what it is like to be a scientist in America in a time when science has become a form of established religion, and scientists its priests and ministers." [9]

This glorification is not merely a diffuse cultural backdrop for professional science, but is also characteristic of the policy-making nerve centers of government. Deference to "science" helps to generate a bullish demand for specialized expertise. As one political scientist observes from his experience in Washington: "Policy makers, legislative and administrative, in the faith that every problem can and should be solved (they have seen it happen in the physical world) turn to social scientists and ask for similar results on social problems." [10]

All kinds of scientific knowledge and expertise are perceived by policy makers, the mass public, and scientists themselves to be relevant to a nearly all-inclusive range of problems, goals, and decisions. Everett C. Ladd observes: "The exponential growth of bodies of expert information, the increased complexity of public problems as they are defined before the society, and the emergence of a large class of high status 'brain workers' committed to the styles and orthodoxies of rationality and expertise, elevate science to the status of a principal ideology offering systematic analysis and prescription as to the issues of public life." [11]

In this context, "knowledge" becomes a product to be distributed, and its production is often tailored to the needs of "consumers." While knowledge for its own sake is still sought, it is the development of "applied" knowledge that dominates the "knowledge market." [12] American universities are very much the knowledge factories of the knowledgeable society.[13] Their intimate and extensive ties with primary consumers of applied knowledge in the federal government and in industry not only form the demand-supply networks of this market but also shape the substance and quality of what is produced, for in large measure these ties pose the problems to which knowledge is perceived to be most relevant, and, furthermore, influence the ways in which it will be pursued and employed.

In his characterization Lane treats "knowledge" as a rather uniform commodity producing fairly constant results, one of which is the displacement of "ideology." [14] He neglects Robert Lynd's classic question to the social sciences: *Knowledge For What?*.[15] In fact, divergent definitions and certifications of knowledge, its demand-supply dynamics, and its varied political consequences render its role far from uniform. Varieties of knowledge and varied perceptions of it combine to generate a myriad of actual and potential uses.

Perspectives such as Lynd's, which recognize the importance of culture and perception in shaping the pursuit of knowledge, are in the classic tradition of the sociology of knowledge.[16] The recognition that intellectual milieu influences the very definition of "knowledge" is conducive to viewing the latter as a political resource and as the product of a political process. In this sense, Lane's description of "knowledge" as encroaching upon "ideology" neglects the politics of both ideology and self-interest that often attend the production, distribution, and uses of "knowledge."

The demand for knowledge by clients and consumers is often highly political in origin, thus politicizing the goals for and conduct of knowledge production. Nor is the political dimension confined to external pressures from the larger system, for the professionalization of an academic discipline gives a new intensity to the internal politics of an occupational group by creating new and enlarged self-interest stakes and more occupational resources to be selectively distributed.

In the knowledgeable society there is a potential political use for any scholarly commodity that may in some manner be termed "knowledge." [17] The nature and consequences of use and the locus and benevolence of the users is problematic. Edgar Litt has observed that in postindustrial society "the instruments of knowledge are in constant tension, the broadest dissemination of skills and ideas is balanced against the restraints of government and the managerial elite. Knowledge becomes both a resource for human liberation and a primary device to ensure social control among agitated masses."[18]

The political consequences of knowledge are primarily determined not by its inherent and immutable characteristics, but by the perspectives and goals of those who create and use it.[19] Recognition of this has led to a renewed concern for its role in democracy. Edward Shils, for example, has voiced the fear that vast accretions of data made instantly available in a federal data system may be prejudicial to both democratic processes and the psychic freedom of individuals.[20] Thus the question "Knowledge for what?" is inherently political as well as epistemological.

The characteristics of the knowledgeable society make knowledge an important political and public policy resource. The complex and technical nature of problems in all areas of domestic and foreign policy coupled with the public affect for science and knowledge render the use of "expertise" an unarticulated premise of policy making at the national level. Regardless of the dynamics or consequences, it is certain that "expertise" is no longer merely an adjunct to policy decisions, but, instead, lies at the core of the decision making process.[21]

Because definitions of "knowledge" and perceptions of its capacities and limitations are relevant to its consequences, consideration of how we know what we claim to know is crucial in analyzing its actual and potential political effects. The "knowledge" that scientific professions impart to consumers is, in a very real sense, shaped by professionally dominant epistemologies. The scientific philosophy (or epistemic preferences) of political science must be examined in order to discover how it determines which of its inquiries deserve to be thought of as "knowledge," and thus deserve serious consideration by clients and publics.

Even in the knowledgeable society, the "objective standards of veridical truth" to which Lane refers are not fixed or self-evident. They are, instead, the product of a dynamic interaction between scientific philosophy and the sociology of knowledge; between the prejudices and ideologies mortal men bring to the pursuit of knowledge and the reasoned mechanisms, constructs, and procedures by which they seek to exorcise or control such biases.[22]

The operational balance between these conflicting influences arrived at by a scholarly discipline structures the production and use of "knowledge."

From this analytical perspective, the existence of the knowledgeable society raises more questions than it answers concerning the nature of knowledge and its relationships to politics.

III

The Professional Milieu:
Its Nature and Consequences

In his classic work *Social Theory and Social Structure,* Robert K. Merton observes that intellectuals have failed to perceive the conflicts and influences associated with their role and have neglected the introspection by which these might be illuminated.[1] He exhorts intellectuals to pose some probing questions about themselves and their milieu: Who defines their problems? What are the effects of bureaucracy upon their perspectives? Are their alternatives restricted? Where are the existential and social bases of mental endeavor located, and how do these bases shape mental processes. What are the cultural bases of definitions of objectivity? What alignments of social interest are relevant to the sociology of knowledge?

The structures and processes of professionalism are a key variable in the sociology of knowledge as applied to the knowledgeable society. While many scholars have hinted at its relevance, the study of professionalism as an independent variable has been severely neglected. It is usually approached indirectly, without proper emphasis upon its autonomous capacity to influence the subjective orientations of professionals and the nature and output of their work.

In tracing the development of professionalism, three types of occupational evolution culminating in professional status may be discerned: the medieval origin of certain classical professions, the later and continuing movement of low-order occupations into professional status, and the relatively recent emergence of scientific disciplines to professional stature.[2] Developmental patterns that are in some sense common to all three provide certain generalizable insights about the nature of professionalization. These serve as an ideal conceptualization of the profession as a mode of social organization.

The basic structural characteristics that define the profession as a distinct pattern of social organization and behavior may be simple or complex. In the former case, the societal mandate for professional identity may consist of little more than lay deference to professional expertise within the particular sphere of work. Professional identity of the simplest sort still demands a modicum of group awareness, of social and occupational identity. This in turn provides the impetus for the development of a professional organization, through which awareness and identity are operationalized. The primary goal of such organization is to establish patterns of social integration and differentiation favorable to the preservation and enhancement of professional self-interest within the larger social system. Public perception of the legitimacy of "professional" claims is a crucial variable in determining their viability.

The mechanisms that foster a professional structure and process are numerous, but the most decisive is dominant control over entry. Total control, which would be ideal from the perspective of professional organization, identity, and unity, is rarely, if ever, achieved, especially in egalitarian societies. Usually, some form of licensure, certification, training process, or other performance standards or selective criteria serve to provide the minimum of entry control necessary for professional stature. These mechanisms may be formal, informal, or a mixture of both. The latter is usually the case, since the profession is a social "group" whose characteristics include both primary group and secondary group features and fuse formal and informal elements. While entry control has many ramifications, its basic function is to differentiate the status and identity of the profession vis-à-vis other occupational groups and the larger society.

Entry control usually involves some definition of the terms of entry and a subsequent shaping of career channels and hierarchies so as to produce an effort-mobility structure culminating in professional status. This usually demands an early and sustained commitment on the part of the aspirant. Once a basic demarcation of the profession has been achieved, its relationships with society must be defined. Most modern professions realize this through the "service role," which characterizes the profession as employing its expertise for the benefit of, or on the behalf of, others, whom we may loosely classify as "clients."

Some definition of "clients" and some prescriptions for relationships with them are necessary for an effective organization, but the substance of such definitions has consequences transcending organizational utility. Everett Hughes has perceptively observed that both professional arrangements concerning licensing and the nature of the mandate that society imparts to the profession may actually reflect the moral "division of labor" within a society, as well as the occupational one.[3] Definitions of "client" and "service" relationships allocate moral rights and responsibilities in a manner determined not solely by the inherent logic of occupational efficiency, but also by the configuration of cultural values. The priest may be delegated the right to elicit and possess "guilty knowledge" concerning the morality of his "clients," but in an extremely secularized society, the same functon might nstead be delegated to the psychiatrist.

In the most modern, technologically advanced societies, the definition of the esoteric "service" performed by the profession is usually based upon a science or a combination of several sciences.[4] This gives new dimensions to the historically common mechanisms by which the identity of professions has been achieved. The functions of a shared language and terminology, which have historically been sources of unity, identity, and structural differentiation for professions, have become even more significant as the professional foundation tends increasingly to be "scientific." The characteristics of a "science" render it extremely congruent with professionalism. For example, scientific degrees serve as ready-made certificates of entry and the practical utility of scientific knowledge helps to define a "service" role.

Having established itself, the profession uses its newly defined relationships and status to enhance its internal solidarity. The inception of a profession and its postnatal drive toward solidarity foster shifts in the subjective orientations of professionals and aspirant professionals with regard to reference groups and values; the profession and its attendant norms become the dominant occupational frame of reference. The judgments and values of laymen, and even clients, become secondary reference points. The profession's standards and the preferences of its members, acting as an occupational peer group, become the litmus test for moral and technical judgments within the occupational sphere.

Once established, the profession becomes a primary mechanism for the allocation of rewards and sanctions. Formerly, such a role may have been played by the local organization or institution or simply the larger society (if the occupation role was very nebulous). Lay and client judgments and consumer demands for services played a more prominent role in determining the occupational fate and prestige of individuals and groups prior to the emergence of full-fledged professionalism. Loyalty also shifts, away from the particular organization or institution within which the professional works and toward broader "professional loyalties," generating potential conflicts with patterns and priorities in the immediate work context. For the academician, this may mean primary loyalty to the profession and to the department, with intermediary occupational allegiances being largely abandoned.[5]

Professionalization provides a status that replaces many of the functions of social class or other status categories. David Reisman offers the perceptive notion that academic life is capable of rapidly declassing those who enter it by severing traditional class ties with family, religion, and ethnicity.[6] This is especially true of academicians from lower-class, minority-group, or rural backgrounds. Reisman contends that for such dislocated persons, the profession becomes a primary reference point that to some extent fills their status and reference vacuum. It functions as a status niche whose outward appearance in terms of material rewards and life style approximates that of a comfortable upper middle-class position. An academician—or a professional in general—need not be dislocated, in Reisman's terms, for the profession to have for him an important status function. An upper middle-class background compatible with professional status in terms of life style may still allow a more subtle kind of "dislocation" by which professional values and orientations replace those of upper middle-class lay culture. Moreover, the individual-istic nature of academic endeavor and achievement tends to atomize the individual, thereby increasing the profession's potential influence as a reference group.

In general terms, status assigns persons to various social categories, implying certain rights and duties, which help to shape an individual's self-conception.[7] The idealization of professional status as a symbol of upward mobility and success makes its influence upon self-conception even more potent. C. Wright Mills describes what he terms the "status panic" in the white-collar world, resulting in a "mock professionalism" for nonprofessional positions that relieves status insecurities created by the death of the Horatio Alger myth.[8] The push-pull effect of status insecurity on the one hand and the desirability of professional status on the other provides professionalism with extensive inroads into self-conception.

Like most large-scale organizations of any type the profession possesses an organizational motivation to control, and to monopolize if possible, the definition and allocation of status, based upon its desire for organizational growth and survival.[9] Status allocation is a crucial means by which organizations preserve their authority over their membership and the position and interests of their leadership.[10] The deference and orientations demanded by a profession's status system greatly influence (and often circumscribe) occupational behavior and cognition.

In their study of American chemists, Strauss and Rainwater found status concerns to be central to professional orientations.[11] The chemists were worried about their relative status within the occupational hierarchy of society. They desired more effective public relations efforts by their professional association, through the dramatization of positive contributions. The researchers discovered a marked consensus among chemists concerning perceptions of their comparative public status. They manifested a status anxiety over what they perceived as a sudden influx of "second rate talent" into their ranks, and also feared a possible restructuring of the professional status system through government interference in industrial research. Strauss and Rainwater suggest that in any profession the membership's perception of status deprivation with regard to public image functions effectively as a source of internal solidarity and organizational stability. In such cases, anxiety and disaffection can be directed outward rather than inward.

Another salient dimension is the role of "professional." Role may be described as the basic allocation of function through codified expectation.[12] A role contains prescriptive norms and guidelines for behavior for persons of a social category. While it permits varying amounts of creative interpretation, the substantial number of norms and prescribed behavior patterns necessary to turn a social category into a role assures that the demands and expectations of "role" will be sufficient to shape significantly the role-occupant's behavior.

One important characteristic of roles is their complementary nature: A role is usually defined and structured by complementary roles, rendering them interdependent. In academia, the complementary role for those of writer and scholar is provided to varying degrees by the professional organization, through its activities and media of communication. Because rewards and sanctions are typically applied by occupants of complementary roles, expectations develop that generate anticipated reactions among role occupants.[13]

It is of vital interest to a profession to obtain a structuring of roles favorable to its interests, and to that end it will seek to create complementary role definitions that protect and enhance its importance to society. Roles also shape the substance and direction of endeavor. If the vast majority of political scientists were to conceive themselves primarily as critical intellectuals rather than as researchers, and were to operationalize this self-conception in role performance, the substance of the discipline's professional culture would be immensely different.

Since roles vary in their status and esteem, public perception of role is a basic factor in determining the magnitude of prestige commanded. Therefore, the profession has a high stake in cultivating a consistent and highly regarded public image of its role, and will usually attempt to cast itself in the most idealized and prestigious role available to it. Strauss and Rainwater discovered that chemists were unable to effect a consistent public image because the variety of roles which they performed had given rise to a host of public and client role perceptions.[14]

Some type of conflict is usually inherent in any role, and it is most often manifested in two conflicting roles performed concurrently by one person, conflicting norms within a single role, or a personality-role incompatibility. Such conflicts can be reduced or eliminated by abandoning certain aspects of role or the role itself. Also, conflicting norms or roles may be separated in the mind of the role occupant through cognitive compartmentalization.[15]

Classic examples of role conflict abound. The role of critical intellectual may conflict with that of scientist; norms of a professional role may conflict with other norms concerning political activism. The degree of actual conflict depends upon the nature and intensity of the stimulus, the subjective perceptions of the role occupant, and his capacities for conflict reduction.[16] Mechanisms for reducing the psychological stress inherent in role conflicts often evolve into the role itself and become standard elements of professional socialization. The surgeon avoids the confusing effects of empathy with his patient through an object orientation toward him that reduces emotional involvement and facilitates the smooth performance of technical functions. Similarly, the political scientist may avoid ideological conflicts or implications of his research through the concept of "value-free" inquiry.

Within a profession, role conflict can exist at collective levels.[17] Resolution or continuing conflict at one level tends to create a similar situation at the other level. A profession whose societal role is nebulous, whose field of endeavor gives rise to several distinct roles, or whose idealized role generates conflict with other social roles finds it difficult to provide its members with a stable and psychologically satisfying professional identity. When the membership contains a vociferous or large component holding self-conceptions that conflict sharply with the dominant professional role, it becomes difficult to maintain the viability of that role. A professional organization confronted with such a threat is inclined to use all available formal and informal mechanisms to reduce role conflict.

Like most organizations, the profession adopts certain norms by which it characterizes itself. It then seeks to transmit and enforce them through compliance induced by the allocation of rewards and sanctions and by the socialization process. The substance of such norms is derived from a wide range of sources including culture and society, clients, the membership, and the professional organization itself. These norms are not the embodiment of ethics that are inherent in a sphere of occupational endeavor, but are instead more validly conceptualized as the result of an interest group competition within that sphere. They reflect the preferences and ethos of a profession's dominant interests, and can be transformed or cast aside as the configuration of these interests changes.

There are several generic norms of modern professionalism that apply to some degree regardless of the particular context.[18] While the role of client is typically devoid of prerequisite norms, there are usually some norms governing client-professional interaction in the service relationship. For example: communication is most often privileged; there is no transfer of skill or technique from professional to client; the decisions or counsel rendered by the professional are limited to a particular sphere of expertise and to a specific period of service. At a more concrete level, the values, internal dynamics, and societal position of a profession help determine content.

A profession usually develops a terminology that codifies occupational reality in a manner supportive of its values and premises. This then becomes a predominant reference point for the membership. The "language" of a profession may be highly scientific and technical, but the fact is that different semantics may codify the same reality in a variety of ways, contingent upon different values, assumptions, and perspectives. Even in a scientific community, terminology is not strictly determined by the inherent characteristics of the phenomena studied.[19]

Identity and symbolism are two closely related elements in the psychological dynamics of professionalism. Individual identity is cultivated in a variety of ways, ranging from the selection process, which may involve a conscious or unconscious screening of potential members according to their predisposition for professional identity, to socialization, one of the functions of which is the inculcation of values and identity. Symbolism facilitates the cultivation of identity and helps to sustain it once developed. As with any subcultural system of belief and behavior, the profession contrives symbolic constructs supportive of its self-definition and image.

The symbolic function of the legend of Florence Nightingale within the nursing profession provides an illustrative example of the dynamics of professional symbolism.[20] Two competing factions each reconstruct the legend to render it congruent with their interpretation of the profession's proper role and image. The constituencies of the two factions are provided by hospitals on the one hand and universities on the other. Hospitals and hospital-controlled training programs have an orientation different from that of the universities, which provide nurses with a broader educational experience. The university image emphasizes the well-rounded woman complete with family; the hospital schools hold a more traditional, spartan image of sacrifice and dedication. Each faction attempts to socialize its students to an image of the Florence Nightingale legend that fits its interpretation of the proper role.

In his work a professional is likely to have the profession's perspectives and prescriptions reinforced by a peer group. This group usually has elements of both a primary group (daily, face-to-face contact on the job) and a secondary group (peer reference through indirect communication, such as professional journals). The influence of the professional peer group need not be severely handicapped by a lack of continuous face-to-face contact if the individual regards the profession as his primary occupational reference point, for he may then internalize its values and experiences. In such cases, the peer group can induce conformity by expectation and anticipated reaction.

In order to illustrate the significance of professionalism, the flow of influence has been described as largely one way: from the profession to the member. Not only do roles present varying degrees of latitude for idiosyncratic behavior and interpretation, but the structured aspects of professional roles, norms, and values are constantly modified as they flow from the collective level to the individual level. They are filtered through the individual's maze of prejudices, beliefs, and psychological defense mechanisms as well as through various impediments that distort communication. Each member develops a somewhat personalized conception of professional role, shaped by his interaction with clients and colleagues, his institutional affiliation, and a myriad of other factors that are to some degree unique. Still, the profession is able to produce and sustain considerable uniformity of belief and behavior among its members. If it could not, it would have difficulty surviving.

Professionalism in American Society

The complexity, specialization, and interdependence of the knowledgeable society have accelerated the rise of professionalism to the point where it has become the dominant mode of organization and orientation at the higher occupational strata. This rise has been aided by the public prestige that it commands.[21] It is not the numerical strength of "professional" types that produces the most significant consequences in the knowledgeable society, but, rather, the orientations of both professionals and nonprofessionals toward "professional" role and status. The most important of these is the widespread and often uncritical deference accorded "professionalism."

The pervasion of the rational, bureaucratic style of organization (in the Weberian sense) has given further impetus to professionalization.[22] The profession is, at base, a bureaucraticized variety of occupational organization. As such, it shares many of the characteristics of Weber's bureaucratic ideal. Both owe their extensive development to modernity; claim to be predicated upon rationality and expertise; and depend upon hierarchy and authority to function and to preserve their self-interest. Though the substantive bases and manifestations of these characteristics differ among various kinds of organizations, the patterns of behavior induced by bureaucracy in general and the profession in particular share certain similarities, due to common structural features.

In twentieth-century America, professionalism is historically unique in its intensity and scope, as are the technological progress and societal complexity that fostered its rise. These more tangible influences are reinforced by—and closely linked to—the cultural infrastructure of the knowledgeable society, which bestows upon professionalism an almost absolute legitimacy and an intrinsic desirability. This cultural regard is an important part of the professional milieu. It appears likely that there exists an image of the "professional," probably widely held, that attributes to him positive traits and functions similar in import and esteem to those attributed to the frontiersman or the Horatio Alger-type entrepreneur. The professional may well be the emerging folk hero of middle-class American culture, or may already be such.

This analysis is primarily concerned not with the evolution of traditional professions but with the emergence of new ones within academia. These more recent claimants to professional status have not received sufficient attention from the sociology of occupations, or from academicians working within them.

Professionalism in Academia

Reisman and Jencks describe the "academic revolution" largely in terms of increased professionalism. They perceive the major consequence of this trend to be a "nationalization" of academic standards. The local institutional setting, with its accompanying religious, ethnic, class, and sectional prejudices, is displaced by a nationalized meritocracy.[23] They assert that this exorcising of parochialism is beneficial because the nationalized standards of admission and education bring increased competence to academia. In addition, professionalism is depicted as increasing faculty autonomy, functioning as an insulator against the incursions of administrators, trustees, and publics who might curtail intellectual freedom. The conflict generated by professionalism's role as a bulwark of academic freedom depends, in part, upon the degree of incompatibility between it and the social and political subculture of the local institution.

Reisman and Jencks document the strengthening of university ties to the occupational structure by describing the proliferation and ascendance of "the professional schools." They are careful to point out that the idealized era of liberal education for its own sake is merely a nostalgic myth and probably never existed; even in colonial times, the student was most often an aspirant minister rather than a lover of pure learning.[24] The question, according to them, is not "whether" American institutions of higher education mixed vocational-professional training and academic pursuits, but, rather, "how" they did so. The novel condition of the "academic revolution" is the magnitude of professionally oriented training, not its existence.

The professionalization of academia and the trends associated with it have not escaped penetrating criticism. C. Wright Mills contends that the universities' independence and creativity have been absorbed by the social system, due to the new modes of scholarly endeavor stimulated in great measure by increased professionalism. Critics like Mills fear that the university has become a conservative institution in which the impetus toward progressive change and innovation is smothered by the bureaucratization of the intellectual role within a professionalized knowledge market.

Mills depicts the rise of the academic entrepreneur, who sells packaged knowledge just as the pharmacist sells packaged drugs.[25] The occupational behavior of this new academic type is much like that of his professional counterparts in industry. Many of the problems of "efficient" management and production, involving resources, staff, and overhead, have become analogous in both spheres. The psychological demands of this entrepreneurial academic role are much like those of the "go-getter" in small business or the executive in the corporation. Mills fears that an academician can play the entrepreneurial role through structural gamesmanship (i.e., the setting up of an institute) and executive ability (in the corporate sense of interpersonal manipulation and management skills) without being aware of the intellectual and ideological implications of his work, and without possessing any goal transcending the role played.

Professionalism is intimately related to (and is sustained by) other trends in the "academic revolution." One of these is the increased permeability among university, government, and corporate structures. The demand for academic "consultants" and the dominance of bureaucratic structure in all three spheres make mobility among them both necessary and feasible.[26] This situation enables an increasing number of academicians to hold a professional self-conception founded upon a "service" role.

The national market for academic expertise is sustained by the knowledgeable society and by its ethos of applied knowledge.[27] In his *The Production and Distribution of Knowledge in the United States,* Fritz Machlup portrays the university as the nucleus of a vast "knowledge market" whose networks of production and distribution extend throughout industry and government.[28] The "production" of knowledge, a term employing the application of knowledge in technological innovation as its frame of reference, is analyzed in terms of "efficiency:" the quantity and quality of the "product" compared to the resources used in production. Economic concepts such as "allocation," "investment," "distribution," and "marginal utility" are used to elaborate the market concept. Machlup depicts the "knowledge industry" as unique and not entirely susceptible to the classical economic analogy, but this uniqueness in no way encompasses the university's traditional role as a center of intellectual criticism and non-technological creativity.

In *The Uses of the University,* Clark Kerr glowingly refers to Machlup's concept of the "knowledge industry" as part of the unique transformation of the American university that has rendered it an institution worthy of emulation.[29] His value premises concerning the role of the university are like Machlup's but less oriented toward economic concepts. To Kerr, the university is, and should be, "service oriented." He views the university-federal government partnership as intrinsically desirable because it is "enormously productive"—again in the sense of applied technology. Kerr assumes an ideal compatibility between the goals of the university and the federal government. Both Kerr's and Machlup's analyses implicitly doubt the utility of criticism and dissent, which are seen as potentially disruptive to the "knowledge industry" and to the service relationships of the "multiversity" that give primacy to applied science.

The ethos of the "multiversity" and the "knowledge industry" lends strong support to professionalism in academia. These concepts are at once both descriptions of the realities of the university's present role and ideologies of knowledge and power that attempt to mold reality to their prescriptions. They help to create and sustain professionalism by serving as justifications for its presence and expansion, and by depicting the trends that foster it as highly productive and desirable.

IV

American Political Science: Profile of an Academic Profession

This chapter highlights some salient manifestations of professionalism in contemporary political science. The purpose is not to assert that professionalization has determined everything that has happened to the discipline, nor is it assumed that the trends described serve only professionalism per se. The web of influence generated by conditions existing within the discipline itself, academia, and the knowledgeable society is extremely complex. The degree to which professionalism is a dependent or independent variable in any of these contexts is problematic, but the purpose here is to demonstrate that political science is significantly professionalized.

Membership

One of the marks of a profession is that its membership becomes specialized, skilled, and certified in a manner that provides a distinct occupational identity and creates lay deference. The trends in the membership characteristics of American political science have been congruent with this facet of development. First, there is the exponential growth of membership, which serves professionalism by providing a scholarly community large enough to support the number and variety of specialized scholarly interests now manifested. In comparison to the discipline's meager membership during its formative years, a mass scholarly audience and occupational peer group now exists.

Increased membership provides the base for a fairly elaborate professional organization. Moreover, the sheer size of this base necessitates (from an organizational viewpoint) the rise of professional elites, who for varying periods and in various capacities give disproportionate attention to the governance and operation of the American Political Science Association, in contrast to the rest of the membership. A larger membership also provides a more durable and effective audience for scholarly elites, whose work becomes the most reputed and most demanded within their sub-fields or within the profession as a whole.[1]

The increased specialization of political science has brought it far from the limited, rather parochial interests of its early history, which were largely confined to Western, democratic institutions and constitutions. An Association survey found that there are now twenty-seven distinct fields of specialization, ranging from personnel administration to foreign policy.[3]

Professional solidarity is fostered by the dominance of the doctorate and the academic career within the Association's membership. In 1974 a survey of 1,000 members revealed that 62 per cent held Ph.D degrees[4] and 77 per cent were affiliated with postsecondary educational institutions. Membership character-istics and employment data garnered from the survey[5] are in-cluded in the second table on page 28.

Even the figures in the table fail to portray the ascendency of the doctoral degree and the academic role. Professional culture is dominated by academically affiliated Ph.D.'s graduated from or working at the most prestigious institutions.[6] This is by no means surprising, for in the period 1958-1965 the eighteen most pres-tigious departments produced 53 per cent of the total doctoral output.[7] Institutional prestige of the school at which the docto-rate is taken is perceived by the membership as second only to volume of publication as a factor in career success.[8]

The journals, annual meeting, and doctoral programs are preponderantly oriented to academic political science rather than to other membership vocations such as journalism or govern-ment service. The academic role constitutes the principal pro-fessional image. Its preeminence is preserved and enhanced by the growing necessity of the Ph.D. degree, which functions as the gate-keeping and certification instrument and as a conduit of up-ward mobility to the elite ranks.

Dominant indices of prestige, especially institutional affiliation

APSA TOTAL MEMBERSHIP ALL CATEGORIES[2]

Year	Number of Members
1903	45
1915	1,462
1925	1,563
1935	1,854
1945	3,466
1955	5,526
1960	7,331
1965	12,311
1970	17,408
1973	16,102
1974	15,631

APSA MEMBERSHIP SAMPLE CHARACTERISTICS

Age	%	N	Employment Status	%	N
20-24	5%	24	Employed Full-Time	79%	414
25-29	24%	129	Employed Part-Time	8%	43
30-34	23%	123			
35-39	14%	76	Unemployed	3%	15
40-44	11%	60	Student	8%	42
45-49	8%	40	Retired	2%	12
50-54	7%	39			
55-59	4%	20			
60-64	1%	6			
65-69	2%	8	Principle Employer		
70 +	1%	5			
			College, University	75%	363
			Community College	2%	8
Sex			Elementary, Secondary School	3%	12
Male	88%	465	Federal Government	5%	26
Female	12%	64	Other Government	5%	22
			Military Service	1%	5
Highest Degree			Private Industry, Business	3%	13
B.A., B.S.	7%	39	Non-Governmental Research		
M.A., M.S.	28%	149	Institute	3%	13
Ph.D.	62%	324	Journalism	1%	3
Other	3%	15	Other	4%	17

of both current employment and doctoral study, give professional
elitism a cumulative quality. The academic role and the Ph.D.
shape professional culture but the prestige departments exercise
an influence upon this role and upon the degree process disproportionate to their size. In this way, the elites who greatly
affect the substance and direction of the profession are, in terms
of career prestige, the elect of the elect.[9] Moreover, the preeminence of behavioralism gives Association governance and professional role an even more sharply defined and cumulative

character. The elected officialdom is increasingly behavioral in scholarly orientation, and the membership perceives behaviorally oriented studies as producing the profession's most significant work.

As is typical of professional careers, "certification" is a long and involved process demanding heavy commitments of time and effort on the part of the aspirant. A survey of 1968 Ph.D. recipients shows that the median time lapse from the baccalaureate to doctorate degrees was 8.7 years, a median of 4.9 of which were spent in registration at a university. The median age was 29.2 years.[10]

Recruitment and Socialization

How do political scientists become such, and in what manner are they trained and inculcated with dominant professional values? Studies of recruitment to graduate school have determined that the process is less than rational and effective. For example, William Buchanan found that recruitment and selection were quite haphazard, due both to the dearth of information received by students about available choices in programs and departments and to the variety and apparent arbitrariness of the criteria of selection employed by graduate schools.[11]

Marked discontinuities exist in matriculation and curricula. The 1968 doctoral profile shows that only one-half of the recipients began their academic pursuits in political science.[12] The Association committee on graduate entrance examinations concluded that the substance and use of such examinations were in need of major reform if they were effectively to select students. It found the tests to be deficient in demonstrated validity, out of step with graduate education, and too loosely connected to undergraduate preparation in political science.[13] These kinds of discontinuities are exacerbated by the typical influx of a large number of students from undergraduate majors in technical fields and in the hard sciences.

The ideal function of socialization is to overcome such discontinuities of recruitment and to mold competent practitioners. Somit and Tanenhaus describe this process:

"The acquisition of the [Ph.D.] degree requires a long and intensive program of study formally designed to transmit the appropriate knowledge and skills. What also occurs, though, is a process of "professional socialization" whereby a body of beliefs, standards, and concerns is concurrently passed along from the older to the younger generation. The activities and accomplishments most esteemed by the teachers acquire prestige in the eyes of students; issues and tendencies which loom alrge for the masters are almost certain to be stressed in training the apprentices. Doctoral programs consequently mirror in miniature, as it were, the discipline's accepted values and concerns." [14]

The process thus described is, of course, somewhat idealized. In reality, stress and dissatisfaction render it far less effective at transmitting values and smoothing discontinuities.

Dissatisfaction with professional socialization is expressed by those who feel that the level of technical competence produced is not high enough and by graduate students who feel that their experience does not meet their expectations or desires. Complaints of the first type hark back to the traditional ethos of doctoral training that glorifies the productive scholar involved in significant research.[15] Dissatisfaction stems from the belief that the skills and techniques demanded by the behavioral approach are not being cultivated in sufficient quality and quantity by existing programs. After an extensive survey of training practices, James March and Heinz Eulau recommended a shoring-up of research skills through extended technical training at both the graduate and undergraduate levels.[16]

Complaints of the second type are reflected in the survey findings of the Association Committee on Obstacles to Graduate Education. Many graduate students (59 per cent of the sample) were dismayed at the quality of preparation for teaching.[17] While most were satisfied with their career choice (which may indicate the ultimate effectiveness of the socialization process), their greatest discontents were not with their individual careers, "departmental culture," or curriculum, teaching, and training, but with the profession itself.[18] This probably reflects the tension between the intense political concerns of many graduate students and the image of the depoliticized researcher that is now paramount with the ascendance of behavioralism. The committee's report concludes that in many cases the skills taught have little to do with education and actually impede it. That is, graduate students are likely to be socialized to the skills of career "gamesmanship" and "academic manipulation" rather than to those needed for the pursuit of knowledge and for competent teaching.[19]

These tensions are likely to persist as the profession's elites continue to push for an ever stronger commitment to the research orientation, the technology of information, and behavioralism, all of which are somewhat dissonant with the external political concerns of many practitioners and aspirant practitioners. Any socialization process is fraught with stress but the profession's unique relevance to political conflicts probably injects added strain. Even so, surveys of the socialization process yield evidence of a nationalized process whose principal imagery stems from prominent trends and conditions in the profession itself, not from the department or the university. The supremacy of academic occupations, of the Ph.D. degree, and of the behaviorally oriented researcher as an elite model constitute a professional role and culture to which most local arenas more conform than depart from.

Professional Organization

The American Political Science Association (APSA) was formed in 1903. Its inception and subsequent development represent the crystallization of professional consciousness. The founding of a national association was not merely an organizational convenience that left intact the discipline's substance and occupational role; the founding challenged (and eventually displaced) the precedence of graduate departments. The Association reflected a more nationalized and standardized conception of the discipline, and provided a means by which this conception's influence could be realized. The interests of the departments, tied to the colleges and universities, and those of the national organization, tied to the emerging profession, often clashed.[20] While such conflicts still exist, the ascendancy of the national organization and its broader professional orientation is beyond doubt.

The APSA has survived a series of challenges and secessionist movements and has continued to maintain and enhance its position. In the mid-1940's the threat came from a movement to force a merger with the American Economic Association. There have been a number of secessionist impulses within subfields of political science where some scholars felt that the Association did not provide an adequate forum for their particular interests. For example, the American Society for Public Administration has, at times, appeared to offer some competition in terms of professional affiliation. Since its inception in 1967, the Caucus for a New Political Science has now and then both challenged the APSA from within and entertained the idea of seceding from it.

The Association is now in its most prosperous era. It offers an impressive list of services and opportunities to its membership ranging from job placement to international junkets, and, as the survey results below indicate, the membership is, by and large, cognizant of these services and of their importance.[21]

ACTIVITIES OF THE
AMERICAN POLITICAL SCIENCE ASSOCIATION

	Aware of Activities		Importance			No Opinion
	Yes	No	High	Medium	Low	
Annual Meeting	99%	1%	70%	18%	5%	7%
Pre-Collegiate Education	56%	44%	31%	24%	18%	27%
Undergraduate Education	74%	26%	59%	21%	3%	17%
Graduate Education	78%	22%	62%	19%	2%	17%
Continuing Professional Education	53%	47%	48%	20%	6%	26%
Placement	94%	6%	72%	17%	5%	6%
Professional Ethics & Academic Freedom	87%	13%	72%	17%	4%	7%
Status of Blacks in Profession	86%	14%	33%	37%	19%	11%
Status of Chicanos in Profession	80%	20%	30%	38%	21%	11%
Status of Women in Profession	89%	11%	33%	38%	19%	10%
Black Fellowship Program	67%	33%	32%	29%	18%	21%
Abstracting and Indexing Journals and Books	52%	48%	47%	24%	8%	21%
Insurance Programs	87%	13%	15%	28%	44%	13%
Biographical Directory	88%	12%	39%	33%	19%	9%
Career Information for Undergraduates	46%	54%	43%	23%	11%	23%
Congressional Fellowship Program	85%	15%	42%	35%	11%	12%

Charges of undemocratic control by an "establishment" or "oligarchy" persist, but from an occupational perspective, the APSA is at its zenith as a professional organization.

Resources

Resources—financial, organizational, status, and technical— are the lifeblood of a profession. They both shape and reflect its relative standing in society's occupational hierarchy and its vitality within its own occupational sphere. Resource levels shape and reflect membership solidarity, "client" demand, and public prestige. A major trend in the professionalization of political science has been the vast increase in the resources at its command.

Burgeoning aid from the federal government and from foundations produced a rapid expanson of all kinds of resources. The maturation of the behavioral revolution and the enhanced rigor and scientism accompanying it provided the major impetus for this trend by opening up new avenues of access to research funds,[22] culminating in the National Science Foundation's long-awaited recognition of political science as a true behavioral science in the mid-1960's.

By the late 1960's the profession's research funds far outstripped earlier levels. A survey of fifty-one departments found that research expenditures from federal grants and contracts in 1967 amounted to $1,135,000, an increase of 270 per cent over 1962.[23] This is concrete testimony to the heightened recognition by the federal government that political science can and does generate knowledge useful to the solution of its problems. In 1962 foundation support reached the point where, in contrast with earlier decades, the most prestigious political science departments garnered more funds than other distinguished social science departments.[24] This tailed off to a parity in 1967, but the profession has certainly "arrived" in the perception of foundations. However, this arrival must be qualified: it is more accurate to state that some foundations favored selected departments. The Carnegie and Rockefeller Foundations multiplied many times over their support to political science in the 1940's and 1950's, but the Ford Foundation provided about 90 per cent of the grants received from American philanthropic institutions in that period.[25] Moreover, this concentration of beneficence was focused mainly upon a few of the most prestigious departments.[26] From 1959 to 1967, one-half of the $100 million total went to three of these: Harvard, Columbia, and the University of California; twelve of the most prestigious departments claimed 80 per cent.

Nor are the foundations unique in the selectivity of their beneficence, for similar patterns are manifested in federal grants and contracts.[27] Thus, the confluence of the academic role, Ph.D. certification, and affiliation with prestige departments that so heavily influences professional culture and the composition of elites is reflected in and buttressed by the patterns of distributing resources.

Technological resources have also mushroomed, due to the interactions of: the behavioral revolution, the technological advances in the knowledgeable society, and the fiscal renaissance of political science. The Inter-University Consortium, while not an Association-run enterprise, must be considered a major technological resource of the profession—for research, recruitment, and socialization. In a very real sense, it is the training academy of the behavioral approach. Basically a partnership among American and foreign universities and the Survey Research Center at the University of Michigan, it provides a vast network of research and training facilities for behavioral scholarship; almost every major graduate department belongs to the Consortium. It has its own administrative staff and functions as the hub of quantitative research.

Estimates by fifty-one department heads of the replacement cost of research equipment used by their faculty members (exclusive of typewriters and digital computers) reached a mean of $8,160 in 1966; the mean for eight of the most prestigious departments was $21,250.[28] Many departments, especially the most prestigious, have their own data banks and centers, often affiliated with the Consortium and/or the Roper Public Opinion Research Center at Williams College. As one would expect, a survey of university computer centers found that political scientists have vastly increased their time logged on various kinds of computers, to the point where March and Eulau optimistically predict that political science will soon surpass its sister discipline of sociology on this score.[29]

In terms of fiscal resources, the APSA has risen from penury to

APSA DETAILED INCOME REPORT[30]

	1972-73	1973-74	1974-75
Membership			
Regular	179,014	191,035	190,000
Student	39,202	37,889	40,000
Family	485	605	500
Life	100	0	0
Institutional (*APSR* and *PS*)	146,954	137,584	140,000
Total	365,755	367,113	370,500
Grants: Salaries and Overhead	32,757	49,240	50,000
Annual Meeting			
Preliminary Program	9,537	5,565	5,000
Final Program	23.364	20,959	18,000
Registration	31,867	32,847	37,500
Exhibits	28,395	25,850	24,000
Total	93,163	85,221	84,500
Advertising			
APSR	64,106	56,295	50,000
PS	1,025	3,408	1,000
Total	65,131	59,703	51,000
Dividends and Interest	33,451	14,385	30,000
Sales			
Back Issues	10,530	3,860	9,000
Directories	0	0	4,000
Mailing Lists	14,894	22,058	15,000
Panel Papers	9,328	7,323	6,000
Reprints and others	1,542	2,327	1,000
Department Chairmen Lists	0	0	0
Total	36,294	35,568	35,000
Rent	27,828	28,933	26,000
Royalties	9,259	11,010	10,000
Personnel Service	10,586	13,506	14,000
Miscellaneous and Contributions	1,007	2,257	1,500
Total Income	675,231	666,936	672,500

*Additional income projected from Institutional Membership dues.

55,000*

727,500

(1973-74 figures are estimates, 1974-75 are projections)

affluence. As recently as two decades ago it was floundering in severe budgetary crisis. Membership dues, the primary source of revenue, were at best tardy and at worst unpaid. The scarcity of revenue precluded effective liasion with government and the press. A sharp rise in income from dues in the early 1950's made possible the creation of a secretariat that more efficiently managed money matters. Improvement in the Association's financial position came slowly at first, and then, by the mid-1950's, rapidly.

The APSA now boasts a multimillion-dollar treasury. It owns several hundred shares apiece of thirty-five blue chip stocks and holds bonds and invests in savings and loan associations. Its holdings are guided by a resolution demanding that the social consequence of investments be considered, excluding from its portfolio weapons industries or "exploitative" or "discriminatory" employers.[31]

A discussion of resources should not neglect political "knowledge." This constitutes a resource in that it enhances professional status and expands the breadth and quality of its potential service role. In another sense, it is a resource to individual scholars because it enhances their abilities and opportunities to pursue their vacation of studying politics. Finally, it is an important resource in the knowledgeable society, especially to the policy-making centers of government.

Modes of Communication

Communications networks are a prerequisite for any kind of organization, and the universal modes of informal communication involving both primary and secondary group forums are as important to the profession as to other organizations. The university department is the arena of face-to-face contact among professional peers on a day-to-day basis. The trends of modern behavioralism have encouraged group research, which reinforces primary group contact.[32] Secondary group forms of informal communication among professional colleagues (letters, exchanges of scholarly material) are also important.

The central channel of formal communication having the greatest impact on professional culture is that of the prominent

scholarly journals. The journal commanding the most professional prestige is *The American Political Science Review* (APSR)
which began publication in 1906. Throughout its history it has
been the target of intense criticism concerning its editorial practices. This is, in part, a natural consequence of its preeminence,
for it is a scarce professional resource competed for by various
approaches and scholars. Like other respected journals, it distributes not only information but professional repute as well. The
increasingly behavioral orientation of its content has come under
strong fire, and its perceived failure to give sufficient attention
to contemporary problems in proportion to its research articles
has been attacked.[33] Such criticisms indicate that journals are
an arena for contending definitions of professional role and
image. This renders editorial judgments paramount not only in
defining qualitative standards for research, but also in shaping
professional values. Editors and advisory boards function in
part as gatekeepers for the elite ranks.

Despite criticisms, a recent survey found that the typical reader
consumes between one quarter and one half of the APSR, and
that the vast majority of respondents gave the Journal a positive
overall rating.[34]

PROPORTION OF THE AMERICAN POLITICAL SCIENCE
REVIEW READ REGULARLY

	None	Less than ¼	¼ - ½	½ - ¾	More than ¾
Entire Issue	5%	24%	30%	24%	17%
Articles	3%	31%	34%	22%	9%
Association News	5%	24%	23%	25%	23%
Committee Reports	10%	37%	26%	16%	11%
Research/Training Support	7%	22%	23%	21%	28%
Professional Conferences	5%	22%	21%	23%	29%
News and Notes	4%	17%	20%	24%	36%

AMERICAN POLITICAL SCIENCE REVIEW RATING

Excellent	Good	Fair	Poor
23%	47%	21%	9%

As the profession continues to grow and to become increasingly
specialized, the journals proliferate. Since the founding of the
Political Science Quarterly in 1886, well over a dozen journals

geared to the research and teaching concerns of the profession have materialized. Some, such as *Polity* and the *American Journal of Political Science,* published by the regional affiliates of the Association, offer a general fare of articles. Others cater to subfields of scholarly interest: *World Politics* is especially attuned to international relations, *Public Administration Review* and *Comparative Political Studies* to their respective specialties. In general, the newer journals tend to be highly specialized: *Political Methodology, Teaching Political Science, Political Theory.*

Two publications focus particularly upon professional matters. *PS,* published by the Association itself, is a "newsletter" concerned with political science "as a profession and as an academic discipline." It invites analyses of the professional community and reports various activities of political scientists: teaching, consulting, researching.[35] The *Newsletter* of the Caucus for a New Political Science seeks to provide an opposition forum for critical and minority viewpoints, and also serves as the communicative organ of the Caucus.

In addition to journals there are a growing number of series of monographs and professional papers, which are usually geared to a subfield or specialty. They may be purchased individually or in series and have the advantage of transcending the space problems that plague journals, thus allowing the dissemination of manuscripts whose length would be prohibitive for journal publication.

Another channel of formal (and informal) communication is provided by annual conventions and regional meetings. Like the journals, they serve not only as forums for exchange of information but also as mechanisms of professional prestige. Thus they afford similar kinds of influence and draw similar criticisms. In a 1963 survey, 42 per cent of the political scientists responding felt that "there has developed an inner group in the American Political Science Association which, in large part, controls the key panel assignments at the annual Association meetings." [36] Despite some effort at broadening the convention's participatory base, one-third of the total of 1,400 panel chairmanships, discussant slots, and paper presentations from 1962 to 1966 went to scholars from ten of the most prestigious departments.[37]

It is at conventions and meetings that professional elites act out their roles of governance, symbolism, and intellectual leadership. It is here that both knowledge and repute are communicated and distributed in vast quantities. Just as the national party convention conveys to the party faithful the vitality, tradition, and sense of purpose of the political organization, the annual convention—one of the most vivid personal experiences in professionalism that the political scientist can undergo—conveys similar kinds of impressions in an occupational sense.

Professional Politics

The manifestations of professionalism just described do not displace occupational politics, but rather, give it new dimensions. At a broad level, the Caucus for a New Political Science constitutes something of a counterculture whose goal is to reorder intellectual and professional priorities. Groups like the Women's Caucus and Black Caucus concentrate their political thrust on the internal distribution of resources and the equity of professional processes.

Contests and debates about governance have been a constant element in professional politics. In the 1930's and 1940's it was the excessive power of APSA committees, unchecked by the Association's elected officers or membership, that provided the major issue.[38] After a bitter and protracted struggle, committees were stripped of their power and new administrative and representative structures were devised, and set forth in a constitution.

Since its inception, this constitution has been a primary conduit for professional politics, for, like all constitutions, its provisions and mandates affect various interests and factions unevenly. The amendment of 1969 allowing for ballot by mail was adopted only after acrimonious grappling with the perplexing issues of democratic theory. Was this a salutary change, broadening the electorate and giving the membership a greater chance to be heard, or was it—as critics charged—a ploy of counterinsurgency seeking to stifle the real politics of the annual business meeting with a flood of uncritically allegiant support for the Association slate from political scientists who knew too little about issues and lacked sufficient interest to attend the convention?

While the Association and its policy committees have no formal powers with which to control scholarly processes and behavior, the "governing" apparatus is still crucial to professional politics. The intellectual and professional posture of the Association's elected officers significantly influence professional image and tone. The opinions of APSA committees, while only advisory in nature, are intensely debated precisely because they constitute an attempt to establish collective norms and standards—or to set a tone for them—in such important areas as political rights and the ethics of research. Even in purely symbolic terms committee decisions are important. In 1973, a resolution before the committee on professional ethics sought to investigate Dr. Henry Kissinger for possible unethical conduct in his role as advisor to President Nixon. The debate on this resolution, resulting in its rejection, demonstrated that the core issue was enmeshed in competing professional values, and not simply conflicting views on American foreign policy.[39]

V

The Sociology of
Political Knowledge

The sociology of knowledge is an extremely complex and nebulous field. A survey of the issues and problems with which it deals is often more bewildering than enlightening, within the context of a particular discipline.[1] In analyzing the influences of milieu upon intellectual endeavor, the sociology of knowledge frequently becomes enmeshed in highly abstract debates of metaphysics and ontology that are far removed from the tasks of the working researcher. It is a problem of the greatest magnitude that within social science, those who study the development of knowledge and those who are directly involved in its production are, by and large, intellectual strangers. At times the working researcher and the intellectual clinician seem separated by a kind of intellectual apartheid, created by marked differences in styles and goals. These differences, while real and formidable, have led to a professionalized compartmentalization within which many political scientists seem to possess an almost xenophobic hostility toward the sociology of knowledge.

This chapter seeks to relate some of the salient dimensions of the sociology of knowledge to contemporary political science—a crucial intellectual linkage that has been severely neglected, despite the introspective impulses generated by the behavioral revolution and by critiques of it.[2] The analysis argues for a middle-range linkage between the sociology of knowledge and political inquiry, lying between experimental controls at a nuts-and-bolts level and abstract epistemological issues that are contextually divorced from the search for reliable knowledge.

Political science is familiar with the broad paradigm for the sociology of knowledge elaborated by Mannheim, who describes the field as "one of the youngest branches of sociology; as theory it seeks to analyze the relationship between knowledge and existence; as historical sociological research it seeks to trace the forms

41

that this relationship has taken in the intellectual development of mankind." [3]

Mannheim, Weber, and later C. Wright Mills and Robert K. Merton provided more or less abstract analyses of the influences of structure, culture, and belief upon thought and inquiry.[4] One of the most common reactions to these classic expositions of the relationships between intellectual processes and milieu (a reaction certainly not confined to political science) has been to embrace a relativist position.

Relativism is often labeled "anti-scientific" or "nihilistic" by its critics, because its cognizance of the existential bases and motives of "thought" often leads to varying degrees of skepticism about the validity of "science" and "knowledge." Two basic premises of most varieties of the relativist position are:[5] that thought and observation are linked to subjective states of being; and that this linkage bears on the validity of "knowledge."

Carried to their logical extreme or left unqualified, these premises are, ipso facto, nihilistic. They preclude any escape from myth and bias. Indeed, to adopt the relativist position in unqualified terms is to discard the reliability of modern science.

Few scholars would disagree with the relativist assertion that norms are culture bound. This is an empirically validated proposition, not a metaphysical contention. It is also correct (by definition) to view "knowledge" as culture bound in derivation and utility, provided such knowledge does not constitute a general principal or universal law. The problem with a strident relativist position involves the leap from these practical recognitions to the unwarranted conclusion that the logic of explanation and validity of science are, by necessity, completely contextual. For example, A. R. Louch concludes: "Relativism thus means that actions can only be judged in context, and that there happens to be no universal context. Explanations of human action is context bound."[6]

If by "explanation" Louch means nothing more than speculative discourse or conventional wisdom, then he is correct. If instead he means the valid knowledge produced by authentic science, his assertion must be rejected; for if accepted, it would mean that there is no practical difference between science on the one hand and common sense or ideology on the other.

Critics of relativism are fond of attacking its logical flaws. Ernest Grünwald describes one of the most blatant, manifested in a variant of the relativist position that he calls "relationism": a purportedly less extreme form of relativism that claims to lie in a middle ground between relativism and extreme logical positivism, but that actually embraces the same basic assumptions as relativism. "Relationism asserts the view that everything given— this world being taken in the widest possible sense—can be grasped only in perspectives; but this proposition itself is supposed to be valid absolutely, not just for one perspective. In each proposition it advances, relationism is thus obliged to contradict its own thesis."[7] To this the orthodox relativist would probably reply that Grünwald's logic is itself a product of his cultural predispositions. Thus we have come full circle and nothing of use to the practicing researcher or theorist has been evidenced.

The seemingly endless and often circular discourses that characterize the relativist-positivist debate have offered the profession little insight about how to come to terms with its intellectual milieu. If a political scientist embraces one side or the other, it is because he is fond of the semantics or of the logical case in an abstract sense; but it is practically impossible to relate either position to the problems of inquiry in any concrete manner. The unfortunate poverty of intellectual substance that characterizes much of the sociology of knowledge has helped to render it irrelevant to the practical tasks of research. Instead, the area has become a kind of metaphysical sandbox for esoteric scholarship.

How then do working political scientists reconcile the pursuit of valid knowledge with the subjective, parochial biases that the sociology of knowledge describes? There are three basic responses:

• To become so enamored with the power of culture and structure to shape thought that relativism is embraced and skepticism replaces the pursuit of science or objectivity;

• To hold that the problems posed by the sociology of knowledge have been mitigated or even obviated by the scientific method (as practiced by the physical and natural sciences), and to view the task as one of transplanting this "method" to political science;

• To be impressed that there are difficult problems of bias in inquiry that have not been solved ipso facto and in a universal manner by scientific method, but that can be solved by the good intentions of the researcher or theorist in each particular endeavor.

The profession's failure to deal effectively with problems of bias is preordained by the pervasion of these inadequate responses.

The first response logically abjures the pursuit of what is accepted by the natural and physical sciences as "science." The second abjures the sociology of knowledge itself by uncritically assuming that scientific canons of objectivity have rendered it largely irrelevant or anachronistic. This response appears at times to transcend the realm of the secular through its faith in the objectivity of "scientific method." Only the third response finds its way into the actual conduct of inquiry, but its presence is tenuous and symbolic. Like the other two, it fails to enhance epistemological quality and scientific consciouness.[8] This third response has been called "confessionalism."[9] It consists of paying lip service to the problem of bias by touching base with classic works from the sociology of knowledge and then "confessing" their relevance and potency vis-à-vis the subjective orientations of the researcher or theorist. The problem is that while confessional caveats may be cathartic for both writer and reader, they do not enhance the reliability of inquiry. As Paul Kress observes:

"If we understand the author's confessional as a reason to read a report of similar research by a scholar of differing tastes, how are we to choose between them, and what, in any case, has become of the ideal of objectivity? . . . Beyond these objections it might be urged that the confessional strategy promotes a false sense of having somehow 'dealt with' the problem of subjectivity. Articulated sins are always someone else's problem . . . a priest's, a lawyer's or a reader's."[10]

These three responses have a similar influence: each precludes effective links with the sociology of knowledge. Extreme relativism views bias an an unalterable fact of intellectual life rather than as a problem to be solved. The second response assumes that the advent of scientific method solved practically all problems of bias. The confessional approach substitutes clichés for careful scholarly introspection. In describing the incidence of what Kress terms confessionalism, Karl Popper blames the sociology of knowledge itself as a field:

"The sociology of knowledge is not only self-destructive, not only a rather gratifying object of socioanalysis, it also shows an outstanding failure to understand precisely its main subject, the *social aspects of knowledge,* or rather, scientific method. It looks upon science or knowledge as a process in the mind or "consciousness" of the individual scientist, or perhaps as the product of such a process. If considered in this way, what we call scientific objectivity must indeed become completely ununderstandable or even impossible; and not only in the social or political sciences, where class interests and similar hidden motives may play a part, but just as much in the natural sciences. . . . If scientific objectivity were founded, as the sociologistic theory of knowledge naively assumes, upon the individual scientist's impartiality or objectivity, then we should have to say good-by to it." [11]

Despite the inadequacy of responses to the problems posed by the sociology of knowledge, and despite deficiencies in the ways in which the problems have been posed, there are still important benefits to be gained in forging an effective linkage. As a field of analysis offering intellectual insights useful in the behavioral era, the sociology of knowledge cannot be conceived as synonymous with either the history of ideas or the study of cultural ethnocentrisms. At its best, the sociology of knowledge is a source of critical appraisal concerning the methods, theories, and concepts employed by the profession as it struggles for a viable definition of "science." As such, it can do more than trace the evolution of structural-functionalism from sociology to comparative politics, or chide the earlier ethnocentric fixation for Western, democratic systems. It can be linked in a direct, clinical manner to the styles and techniques of inquiry; a linkage that will benefit the political scientist as a practitioner, not merely as a dilettante scientific philosopher or intellectual historian.

The sociology of knowledge is most fruitfully viewed as the

analysis of the roots and manifestations of bias in inquiry. Seen in this manner, it has a very practical and immediate utility for intellectual progress. Berger and Luckman offer a broadened definition of the field that bolsters its clinical potential for political inquiry:[12] "It is our contention that the sociology of knowledge must concern itself with whatever passes for 'knowledge' in a society, regardless of the ultimate validity or invalidity (by whatever criteria) of such 'knowledge' . . . . In other words, we contend that the sociology of knowledge is concerned with the analysis of the social construction of reality." [13]

Anything broadly defined as "knowledge" can be analyzed as a construction of reality. This construction and the methods and criteria by which it is arrived at must be scrutinized to uncover biases and deceptions. This endeavor is not synonymous with elaborating the history of the profession or with cataloguing the myths that it has transcended. Rather, the sociology of knowledge can function as the flip side of scientific philosophy.[14] If the latter sets goals and criteria for scientific inquiry and reliable knowledge, the former deals with biases whose intrusion into inquiry prevents the attainment of what is sought.

The concept of "bias" in political inquiry is frequently associated with notions of value bias elaborated in some of the profession's critical or anti-behavioral literature.[15] Value bias is often perceived in terms of a concern for the injustices of the American political system, and for the ways in which dominant patterns of research relate to them. Discovering biases in the profession's research priorities, clientele, and service roles is a legitimate facet of the clinical potential of the sociology of knowledge, but these areas do not constitute the analytical whole. There exist other biases that are rooted primarily in deficient research methods and epistemology. These are as detrimental to the search for knowledge as are value or ideological biases. In fact, many epistemological biases are spawned by or linked to the collective ideological biases of American political science.[16]

This analysis views "bias" as any influence upon inquiry that results in the perpetuation of ignorance, the creation of self-deception, or the cognitive constriction of reality.[17] Some examples of the kinds of biases that plague research and theory will be offered.[18] Whether these originate in individual or professional value commitments, inadequate attention to methodology and epistemology, or a combination of both, is not important for the purpose at hand. The illustrations attempt to add substance to the contentions that the sociology of knowledge applies to political science and that formidable biases exist.[19]

Conceptual Biases

Concept formation is a vital part of the pursuit of knowledge. Like the language in which they are expressed, concepts are representations of reality. Their utility in a scholarly discipline (especially one seeking to be scientific) is determined in large measure by their objectivity and precision. Concepts help to organize perceptions of empirical reality and to weld them into manageable cognitive entities. They are the building blocks that the researcher juggles, amends, and synthesizes to provide an understanding of phenomena.

A primary goal of science is to guard against concepts that are vague or arbitrary. In order to probe phenomena effectively, concepts must have analytical purpose transcending myth and ideology.[20] How one goes about this in terms of substantive research is a very difficult matter. For present purposes it suffices to say that to the extent that concepts lack precision, they impede the attainment of valid knowledge.

One important source of bias stems from the implicit use of concepts. Are the concepts that structure theory and research included, in explicit and integrated fashion, in the statement of the problem, or are they silent partners, structuring inquiry but not being held responsible for their role? In the latter case the scholar's endeavor is always inconclusive or misleading. The perspective of inquiry is only partially accounted for in the empirical test because implicit use of concepts shapes both the formulation of the problem and the interpretation of results. In such instances the process of inquiry is (to employ an oft-used analogy) much like an iceberg: the explicit portion is only the visible tip of the conceptualization that is crucial to the logic of inquiry; the hidden portion lurks in the depths of unexpressed or subconscious bias, and, sheltered from the light of test and validation, wrecks the validity of theory and research.

In political science the implicit use of concepts is a major problem. As William E. Connolly observes, the selection of concepts has not been justified epistemologically: exacting criteria that place logical checks on selection are most often elusive or non-existent.[21] Connolly employs the notion of a "contrast-model" to depict such implicit uses. In analyzing conventional pluralist theory, he concludes that much of it is integrated and logical not on the merits of self-contained theories and hypotheses under test, but only through the implicit use of contrast-models of authoritarian and totalitarian systems, or of pluralistic arrangements in other societies.[22]

To the extent that the implicit use of concepts shapes the perspectives of research and yet remain unaccounted for by epistemological justification and empirical test, they render political inquiry "other directed" and inherently unreliable. For example, many of the most respected theoretical formulations purporting to explain the *how* and *why* of political development never probe the basic concepts underlying their perspectives of inquiry or their "explanations." One such concept is that of sequential development.[23]

Behind seemingly rigorous formulations involving much quantification and classification lie the intuitive and/or normatively preferential ideas that there is some inherent developmental sequence in the political process: that systems confront political crises in some irreversible order, and that a teleology exists by which Western representative democracy is the ultimate stage of political evolution.[24] While concepts of sequential development shape research perspectives, the construction of typologies, and attempts at causal explanation, they are not themselves specific targets of logical and empirical analysis. Instead, they are often implicitly assumed to be an unchallengeable frame of reference for the study of political development. Such conceptual biases preclude not only "science," but a meaningful understanding of political life. So long as concepts that are crucial to inquiry remain outside the universe of explicit analysis, it is impossible to reach any valid conclusions.

In addition to implicit conceptualization via "contrast-models" in pluralist theory and via the gratifying assumptions of comfort-models in development theory, there exist what are best described as folk-concepts. These are popular representations of reality that, through ideology, political crisis, or intellectual faddism, are thrust into "analytic" use. The problem is that folk-concepts have their origin in other than analytic considerations and are therefore unproductive guides for inquiry. An important reason science differs from conventional wisdom is that it takes the trouble to refine its concepts and trim them down to an explicit, logical purpose. When folk-concepts are smuggled into rigorous inquiry without proper analytical refinement, the distinction between science and valid knowledge on the one hand and myth and speculation on the other becomes marginal or nonexistent.

Such is the case with concepts of "democracy," especially in the field of comparative politics where they enjoyed a spectacular hegemony.[25] The rude awakening that political systems other than Western democracies demanded consideration because they were not aberrations destined to disappear did not hit the profession until the end of World War II. Then, the perceived threat of a Communist domination of underdeveloped areas led to a policy panic over how to quickly stabilize and democratize those areas.[26] Political scientists responded to the intense demand for increased knowledge with impressive quantities of data and theorization. But the prominence of "democracy" as an American policy goal for the Third World led to the use of folk-concepts of democracy that presumed answers to the questions that they were used to analyze. Such concepts continue to shape the theory and research of the sub-field of comparative politics.

Like their folk-concept counterparts, the supposedly "analytic" concepts of democracy were umbrella terms encompassing various configurations of traits most frequently manifested in stable, developed, Western systems. These include: a degree of pluralism and interest competition, regular and freely contested elections, responsive government, a fairly broad distribution of political power, mass participation, and some degree of political liberty. It was simply assumed (probably due to the vitality of the folk-concepts) that "democracy" and its perceived traits were the proper concepts for the study of political development. No scientifically conscious forethought was given to such crucial theoretical questions as:

Are the selected traits the cause or result of a democratic system; are they dependent or independent variables?

Are they universal characteristics of political systems, or the peculiar manifestations of Western democracy?

Are the apparent links between the selected traits and political development real and causal; or are these traits only tangential adjuncts that seem important in historical retrospect because they appear to be cumulative?

The answers were taken for granted, rather than as a primary focus of inquiry. The concept of democracy has been redefined in myriad ways with myriad emphases,[27] but none of these has produced the conceptual refinement necessary for the kind of knowledge sought—at least not in any verifiable manner. Because of the failure to transcend the folk-concept of democracy, there is no epistemological assurance that political scientists have not been quantifying and classifying what are actually spurious characteristics of political development, resulting in a protracted dead-end effort for much of comparative politics.[28]

Cultural Biases

Cultural relativity is one of the most popular notions in all of social science. It is interesting, useful, and easily grasped. As such, it has become the talisman of the confessional approach to dealing with bias. The sociology of knowledge admonishes that intellectual escape from the ethnocentricity of culture is not easy. Culture shapes not only what we think about and the way in which we think about it, but also our conclusions about our thoughts: the standards and definitions of knowledge and falsehood.[29] In the face of very complex problems concerning how the theorist or researcher can transcend cultural biases (or at least avoid outguessing himself), one finds totally inadequate responses. Prefaces of confessionalism that the researcher is a liberal, a Catholic, or a vegetarian lend nothing to the validity of his task.

The sociology of knowledge and its descriptions of the hazards of cultural bias should be neither divorced from political inquiry nor linked to it only symbolically through confessionalism. Instead, it should serve to inform and caution researchers and theorists in every phase of the search for knowledge. The gross intrusion of cultural bias into some of the most advanced areas of inquiry reflects the general failure of the behavioral revolution to employ the sociology of knowledge as a medium of scholarly introspection.

In attempting to probe the relationship between "intelligence" and "sense of political efficacy" in children, one researcher surveyed over ten thousand primary school children. The results were that the variables of sex, social class, school grade, school location, and class participation were all clearly statistically subordinate to "intelligence" in accounting for efficacy levels.[30] "Thus," the author concludes, "children in relatively similar or even dissimilar environments will respond differently to common political stimuli on the basis of differences in individual intelligence."

The problem of cultural (or subcultural) bias lies in the use of standard 'IQ' tests as the measure of intelligence. This is not a tangential problem or a minor methodological oversight, given the researcher's conclusions.

'IQ' tests are not only notoriously culture bound in the broad sense, but are also tied to ideals of achievement and verbal and mental patterns that have been preponderantly associated with America's middle and upper-middle classes.[31] To the extent that the measure of "intelligence" used in this study is biased toward a particular class, does not this readmit the vitality of class as a determinant of efficacy? Since the author concludes that class has "no effect," the possibility is more than a caveat for his findings; it is logical grounds for dismissing them as unreliable. Such cultural biases often find their way into socialization research.[32]

The failure to control for cultural influence beyond those hypothesized often reaches a nadir that strains the imagination. Consider a researcher's conclusion that the unanticipated richness and detail of children's knowledge and image of President Kennedy (discovered in the immediate post-assassination period) was due to the fact that previous studies had underestimated the political competence and knowledge of children.[33] If one abandons the preconceived assumptions that efficacy develops in childhood, that it can be verbalized by children of four to twelve years of age, and that verbalizations possess the meaning for the child's political consciousness that the researcher interprets, there are equally credible explanations of this phenomenon that are not tied to socialization theory.

The researcher reported no effort to determine whether in fact that specificity and detail of the children's responses possessed any *political* meaning for them in the cognitive sense, beyond parental and adult modeling or anxiety reduction. In the cultural crisis of presidential assassination, need there be anything "political" (in any sense relevant to socialization theory) about a first grader's statement that Kennedy's finest contributions involved civil rights progress and the resolution of the Cuban missile crisis? The failure to justify either the moment of inquiry or the interpretation of results leaves the study at the mercy of the cultural trauma and information satiation attending the assassination.

There is no evidence that children saw Kennedy as a "political figure" rather than as a mere "symbol," as the researcher claims. Perhaps the symbolism was simply more intricate and intense and not "political" at all. Surely few educators concerned with the "richness" of technological awareness in primary school children would have taken comfort that specific answers about men on the moon indicated that their charges were being instilled with a catholic curiosity about science.

Another instance of the failure to deal with cultural bias concerns the contradictory results obtained by two inquiries into children's perception of political objects. In contrast to earlier research that had discovered positive and even "beneficent" perceptions, a sample of rural, poor children in Appalachia evidenced a dramatic absence of favorable inclinations toward political objects.[34]. The researchers found no evidence that a process of socialization conducive to regime support was at work in Appalachia. They speculate that the high frequency of positive orientations among children found by other studies may be a culture-bound phenomenon. Furthermore, they assert that because of such variance, socialization theory must work to *explain* political orientations in children rather than merely cataloguing them.

Most socialization theory assumes that regime stability is tied to political culture in a causal manner and that it is in childhood that the crucial bonds of allegiance to the political system are formed. These assumptions are usually not tested, but survey results appearing consistent with them are offered as empirical evidence that the assumptions are correct. The failure to put the assumptions themselves to test, and to control for cultural and subcultural biases, render much research self-fulfilling.

What appear to be culture-wide response patterns are taken as major determinants of system stability and political style rather than as reflections of other dominant influences. The failure to develop or employ techniques that might determine the significance of responses for the children themselves, or the actual "political" content of such responses, injects a superficial façade of universality into findings. This façade is congruent with the largely monolithic and all-determining concept of political culture assumed by much socialization theory. Only culture-wide response patterns can be explained in terms of socialization theory, and only fairly abstract and superficial questions can produce any uniformity of response among children. When the data show a variety of clearly distinct patterns of socialization, the consensus and vitality of culture no longer serve as a convincing explanation for system stability and democratic development. When rural, poor children prove to be an exception to "cultural-wide" patterns, the possibility arises that political culture is a dependent variable, reflecting economic and self-interest positions.[35]

Perhaps the pervasiveness of beneficent perceptions among children is due primarily to the extensiveness of positive economic or self-interest stakes among parents. More simply, perhaps it is due to the authority relationships of the school environment. Assuming that culture is a determining mechanism of the political process, and that any general response pattern that appears "positive" taps the transmission of political culture and the development of political efficacy, conveniently begs the basic theoretical questions concerning the relationships among political culture, political self, and system stability.

Errors of Logical Warrant[36]

The basic problem of logical warrant in political science is the gap between the data gathered or method used and the conclusions reached. Even more serious is the failure to recognize that there is a gap in many instances; that the data, hypotheses, and conceptual precision manifested cannot provide a logical warrant for the conclusions offered.

The problem of logical warrant can be seen in *The Civic Culture*.[37] The study gives the impression of having stated something concrete and valid about the causal roots of democracy,[38] but it is merely a compendium of descriptive, attitudinal data whose causal sequences are circular and whose conclusions about democratic theory are in no way convincingly related to its data through logical theorization and testable hypotheses.

The Civic Culture is a basic example of a descriptive model confusing its assumptions with its explicative capacity. The study is based on the hypothesis that the diffusion of democratic values throughout the population determines the viability of a democratic state. Its conceptual framework, clearly based on British and American precedents, implicitly assumes that democracy and stability are rooted in mass attitudes, and it proceeds to describe political reality from this premise. But the study avoids any concrete and testable exposition of the causal pattern that it takes for granted. Nowhere is there an effort to defend the basic assumptions of inquiry. The independent influence of political culture upon system stability and democratic development is neither the focus of inquiry nor the major hypothesis. It is the basic perspective that structures inquiry and that is simply held to be true.

"The development of a stable and effective democratic government," the authors of *The Civic Culture* state, "depends upon more than structures of government and politics: it depends upon the orientations that people have to the political process—upon political culture. Unless the political culture is able to support a democratic system, the chances for the success of that system are slim." [39]

This kind of statement should be a basic assumption to be empirically validated or a background statement for the development of operational indicators and more specific hypotheses. Instead, it appears at the end of the study and is posited as the major conclusion. The epistemic problem is that this conclusion is exactly like the "approach to political culture" outlined in the first chapter of the work. After describing five political cultures from this approach, the same set of assumptions (still unvalidated by the intervening inquiry) is offered as the conclusion of the study. In the absence of explicit hypotheses and operational constructs that make the assumptions demonstrably contingent on certain empirical conditions, the study becomes an exercise in circular description. *The Civic Culture* combines metaphysical and empirical statements indiscriminately to form deceptive chains of reasoning. Moreover, it manifests an incestuous interplay of empiricism and implicit assumptions.

The point of contention is the study's *ad hoc* approach to the question of political stability. Were the data offered simply as a descriptive comparison of attitudes and values in five nations, there would be no doubt about its scope and richness. But the authors assert that the study was designed to reach a better understanding of the problems involved in the "diffusion of democratic culture," and that it was therefore necessary to develop appropriate measures for that culture and to discover its patterned manifestations in countries with a wide range of experience with democracy. With such knowledge, they argue, "we can speculate intelligently about 'how much of what' must be present in a country before democratic institutions take root in congruent attitudes and expectations." [40] The implication seems to be that rather than providing descriptive material, the authors are probing the causal roots of democratic attitudes and values in such a way as to make it possible to "diffuse" them. It may be that stability *is* the product of certain attitudes and values, but the question remains as to how these came about in the first place. Such knowledge is central to understanding the conditions under which such attitudes and values might be "diffused."

The failure to provide logical warrant is especially notable in conceptual schemata that employ the language of theoretical explanations without basing inquiry on the epistemic prerequisites of such explanation: the formulation of explicit hypotheses, the explication of causal interrelations, and the specification of rules of evidence and correspondence. A prime illustration of this deficiency is Gabriel Almond and G. Bingham Powell's *Comparative Politics: A Developmental Approach,* a lineal descendent of the structural-functional approach and one of the most imaginative and popular conceptualizations of political development.[41] The authors offer a model of political systems that seeks to describe and compare performance of those systems according to classification by their basic structural and developmental features.[42] They circumspectly claim that their schema (1) has moved into the realm of generalization and prediction (p. 322), (2) points toward a theory of political development (p. 322), and (3) implies several basic theoretical relationships (p. 323).

The problem is that the schema, at least in the form presented, cannot logically deliver the theoretical benefits claimed for it because certain epistemic prerequisites are absent: (1) clear and testable distinctions between dependent and independent variables, (2) a theoretical framework positing predictions or generalizations directly relevant to understanding the *how* and *why* of political development beyond an intuitive, descriptive exposition or a mere association of traits, and (3) "statements of theory" that are not analytically barren or tautological. Without these components all that remains is classification via a descriptive model that cannot explain, despite the authors' contention that "the basic theoretical statement here is that the development of higher levels of system capabilities is dependent upon the development of greater structural differentiation and cultural secularization. In a more specifically structural sense, it is predicted that higher capabilities depend upon the emergence of 'rational' bureaucratic organizations. Thus, we predict that a system cannot develop a high level of internal regulation, distribution, or extraction without a modern governmental bureaucracy in one form or another."[43]

Logical warrant cannot be legislated but must be constructed. The "theoretical statement" above cannot offer an explanation of development because of its semantic and conceptual obscurity. The authors specify no propositions for exploring the contention that system capabilities are dependent upon greater structural differentiation and cultural secularization. Nor is it theoretically useful to offer the "prediction" that higher levels of system capabilities necessitate bureaucracy, since this assertion is at best lacking in explanatory significance and at worst tautological. The culmination of this schema in vague generalization instead of truly theoretical statements that could be fruitfully tested and then modified was preordained by the epistemic capacities of a descriptive model, which cannot produce the kind of logical warrant sought—and claimed—by Almond and Powell.

Personal Bias

The values and ideologies that mortal men possess are a serious obstacle for objective research. It is sometimes argued that the other biases described previously are merely manifestations of subjective bias, and this is true by definition. This analysis rejects the conclusion that often stems from this line of argument: that scientific objectivity is primarily a matter of good intention or proper attitude. Posing the problems of bias in terms of the subjective quirks and personal prejudices of the researcher stems almost inevitably not only from the notion that objectivity is synonymous with good intent, but also from the predominantly ideological perspectives from which the problems of bias have been approached.[44] That is, ethical complaints about the values served by research usually lead critics to seek out implicit values and to trace them back to the probable ideology of the researcher. This is not conducive to analyses that seek to discover *how* (by what epistemic shortcomings) implicit values came to distort inquiry. Most often, the starting point of analysis is ideological opposition that, while useful from a muckraking perspective, renders epistemic problems a tangential concern, or of no concern.

The Necessity of Introspection

The profession's ability to assess its progress in the search for political knowledge—however that knowledge may be defined or sought—has suffered from its failure to link up with and apply the intellectual perspectives broadly associated with the sociology of knowledge. This analysis does not contend that the kind of scholarly introspection generated by such links and applications would suffice to produce a science of politics; nor would it even begin to solve the numerous epistemological and value problems facing political science. While the sociology of knowledge is not a scientific or intellectual panacea, it can provide invaluable help in assessing the strengths and weaknesses of research methods and approaches.

When biases of the kind previously described find their way into some of the most conceptually advanced and professionally regarded research, something is drastically wrong. It may well be that the enthusiasm for more data and more theory (spawned by momentum of the behavioral revolution) has resulted in a one-dimensional fixation for the production of knowledge that neglects its quality and reliability. One of the barriers between political scientists and policy makers is said to be that the former are concerned with detached, often jargonized, analysis, while the latter are involved in the pressures of political action and public responsibility. Like policy makers operating in the crucible of power, political scientists have been too enmeshed in the intellectual and professional pressures of actually producing knowledge to stand back and introspect[45]—especially when the sociology of knowledge is often more abstract and jargonized vis-à-vis political science than is political science vis-à-vis the problems of policy makers.

At a broad level the goal is one of crafting and customizing the perspectives of the sociology of knowledge so that they are made relevant to the tasks of political inquiry. It is useless to exhort political scientists to make an effort to link up with the sociology of knowledge if there is in fact nothing comprehensible to link up with. The only clear prescription, other than the need for introspection, is that a wave of superficial confessionalism at both the collective and individual levels must be avoided.

Exhortations for interdisciplinary links—and the responses to such exhortations—too often smack of collective confessionalism. Inviting philosophers, sociologists, or natural scientists to show their wares at our annual convention has about as much impact on scholarly introspection as citing Karl Mannheim on the first page of an article. Of course, intellectual cross-fertilization is indispensable, but it can also be deceivingly cathartic. If outside, clinical help has nothing practical to offer, or if what has practical utility does not find its way into the conduct of inquiry, then interdisciplinary links are primarily symbolic.

In its search for reliable knowledge and its role as a source of expertise on matters of public policy, political science cannot afford to retreat to either confessionalism or a business-as-usual mentality in the production of knowledge. Increased attention to the kinds of perspectives dealt with by that neglected and elusive field, the sociology of knowledge, could provide a fruitful avenue for evaluating the state of both political knowledge and the methods and assumptions that guide its pursuit.

How Do We Know
What We Claim to Know?

This chapter does not attempt to provide an epistemological cookbook for valid explanation. Instead, it develops a middle-range approach to explanation—one dealing with crucial epistemic problems at a level that has generic significance but without succumbing to meaningless abstractions of "grand theory" and ontology that are of no use to practitioners of political science.[1] As Martin Landau points out: "The trouble is that most of the writing in political science on problems of this kind is pitched in such lofty phrases . . . as to obscur the problem under consideration. It is not too harsh a judgment to suggest that bibliographical erudition all too frequently is mistaken for analysis— or that rhetorical grace frequently substitutes for argument."[2]

The specific goals of the approach offered here are several. First, a viable conception of explanation must exclude the kinds of biases depicted in the previous chapter. It must be sufficiently generic and valid to escape the skepticism of the relativist position while at the same time being cognizant of pragmatic concerns about the role of political knowledge in the knowledgeable society. It should also be cognizant of the context of inquiry provided by both the nature of phenomena and the quantity and quality of existing knowledge.

Epistemic Craftsmanship

Epistemic craftsmanship is, at base, a shorthand designation for an approach to attaining valid explanation and reliable knowledge. It is termed "epistemic" because it views as indispensable to the production of valid knowledge the process of reasoning about how we posit or conclude. Moreover, the quality of this process is *the* essential criterion for distinguishing between a demonstrably reliable knowledge on the one hand and ideology on the other. If there exist any patterns of variables or theoretical relationships that can facilitate an understanding of political life in terms meaningful to our goals and experiences, only careful attention to the soundness of reasoning can discover them and separate them from myth or misunderstanding. Without a grasp of the consequence and validity of the reasoning process used in inquiry, there is no effective way to evaluate conclusions. Without careful introspection concerning how we know what we claim to know, the relativist position becomes an incontestable reality.

Linking "epistemic" to the term "craftsmanship" is meant to connote a rejection of the notion of absolute and final solutions to the problems of bias. Just as the intent of objectivity on the part of the individual researcher or theorist is not a real solution to the problems posed by the sociology of knowledge, it is naive to suppose that some neat syllogistic construct can simply be transplanted to political science and thereby both eliminate bias and produce copious amounts of valid knowledge. "Craftsmanship" does not mean that the development of a valid process of explanation is totally relative or contextual or that it is proper for each scholar to develop a new or divergent logic of explanation suited to his subjective goals or substantive endeavors. "Craftsmanship" is not a plea for ad hoc epistemology or for science through serendipity. It simply means that unless logical models or processes of explanation are geared to the phenomena, goals, and scientific exigencies of an area of inquiry, they are likely to be of little use and to be little used. Only when they are contextually meaningful can they do what they are supposed to do: enhance the validity of knowledge.

It is useless to claim an awareness of the context and consequences of political knowledge while playing syllogistic games having no realationship with such concerns, except to preclude their legitimacy. The problem is to develop a mode of explanation that aids the pursuit of valid knowledge—a mode not content merely with generating ideological satisfaction or a rhetoric of scientific rigor. "Craftsmanship" qualifies "epistemic" but does not obviate it.[3] It dictates that a mode or modes of explanation be developed that will be not only sound in the epistemic sense, but useful as well. "Useful" does not mean congenial to preferred values, but refers to increased understanding, whatever the values that that understanding might bolster or depreciate.[4]

Epistemic craftsmanship abjures both sound epistemic reasoning divorced from the important questions facing political science and answers to such questions that reflect needs but neglect the logic of understanding, and that are therefore meaningless as valid knowledge. The detail and substance of epistemic craftsmanship cannot, by the definition employed here, be legislated for the profession, but must be developed. The following discourse attempts to clear away some of the conceptual confusions that have blocked the path to a creditable pursuit of epistemic craftsmanship. To the extent that it is successful, the path may become clearer, but traversing it and rendering it a freeway of science is the job of scientifically conscious practitioners.[5]

The Problems and Context of Explanation

There are two basic categories of problems relating to explanation. The first has to do with the logical character of explanation in general, and will be dealt with in Part II of this chapter. The second deals with the peculiarities of inquiry in political science, or in social science as a whole, resulting from the study of human behavior and cognition. The profession deals with problems and variables that are often as complex and elusive as human nature itself and that are usually viewed as serious obstacles to valid explanation and scientific method. In fact, it is often asserted to preclude them. Some scholars argue that because the study of politics must center upon values, motives, and complex patterns of human behavior, and because researchers necessarily have a great deal of empathy for the phenomena studied, a science of politics is impossible. Most such arguments deem impossible not only the ultimate realization of such a science but also the effective use of scientific methods and approaches.[6]

After surveying all of the major reasons given for the impossibility of an objective or scientific study of social phenomena, Ernest Nagel concludes that none establishes what it purports to establish.[7] That is, while they depict the difficulty of obstacles to be overcome and the complexity of the scientific enterprise in social science, they do not logically preclude scientific activities similar to or analogous to those conducted in the natural and physical sciences. They do, however, raise serious questions about merely transplanting the experimental methods of hard science.

It is generally assumed that the empathy of the social scientist for the human aspects of the phenomena he studies stands in sharp contrast to a research situation involving the study of inanimate objects. This analysis agrees with Nagel that the difference is pertinent to questions about the origin of explanatory theory, but not necessarily to its validity.[8] It is often asserted that such empathy makes objectivity impossible. Yet, this empathy is but one of the many formidable kinds of bias that can intrude upon the validity of inquiry. There is no evidence, or even convincing argument, that this empathy is so strong as to rule out the possibility of objective inquiry through sound epistemology. To hold that this is so is to adopt a relativist position about all social knowledge: a position this analysis flatly rejects.

The other argument about the subjective empathy of the social scientist reaches a diametrically opposite conclusion: that subjective insight is the key to, or necessary prerequisite for, understanding human behavior. This has led to considerable debate about which point of view is most effective in social science, "inside" or "outside." [9] The assumption here is that the goal is the same for both: demonstrable knowledge of phenomena. It makes little difference whether the spark for inquiry comes from empathic insight or objective observation, for valid knowledge cannot be generated by correct attitude alone. The nature of the spark for inquiry cannot assure the validity of inquiry; it is what is done with the objective observation or empathic insight and *how* it is done that will determine whether myth, speculation, or valid knowledge is generated. The tasks of validation are the same for both the "inside" and "outside" perspective; one is superior to the other not inherently, but only to the extent that it can be shown to produce more effectively knowledge and understanding. Such demonstration must, of course, be logical and empirical, and not based on the power of rhetoric alone.

The complexity of phenomena is a challenge to social "science" and not a preclusion of it. It is sometimes contended that the multiplicity of variables in social science, coupled with the conscious capacity of human behavior to alter itself and the conditions that shape it, make broad prediction and generalization impossible, at least in the manner common to established science. Again, the position here is that this is indeed a challenge, but not an impossible one. The case to the contrary often exaggerates the differences between social science and the natural and/or physical sciences in terms of the complexity of phenomena studied. Social scientists tend to underestimate the complexity of the physical phenomena worked with by hard science because they are impressed with the order and relative simplicity imposed upon the physical universe by the working theories and explanations of such science. It may be true that in a total count of relevant variables social science comes out ahead of physical science; the tally has not been made and probably cannot be made. It makes little sense to do so, for the same reasons that the complexity argument itself is less than compelling. It is not the number of variables or the "complexity" of phenomena that really count. It is what we "know" or do not "know" and what we can or cannot "explain" that determine "complexity," as a logical and intellectual factor. To a young child, the alphabet may comprise symbols whose apparent arbitrariness and lack of interrelation is beyond his comprehension. To an older child or adult, the same set is less baffling because its components have been mastered, organized, and usefully employed. So it is with science.

Even in physics—which is often looked upon as the ultimate model for established science—phenomenological complexities abound. In fact, working theories sometimes beg or circumvent such complexities. "Light" is treated as a wave in certain instances and as a particle in others. Such phenomenological problems in established science at least support the possibility that political science may ultimately produce some exceedingly useful and valid theories, based upon aggregate data or marco variables, which work around the complexities of individual motivations and cognitions.

The purpose of theories and explanations is to make useful sense out of jumbles of the phenomenological world. When, as in the physical sciences, much can be explained or predicted, the phenomena studied take on a friendly, even simple, appearance that may mask their inherent or previously perceived complexity. The complexity of social phenomena is so salient in social science precisely *because* viable theories and explanations are lacking. To conclude that social science lacks such theories *because* of complexity is as useful as saying that one's automobile won't run because one doesn't know how to fix it.

The second aspect of the complexity argument concerns those conscious alterations of patterns of human behavior that might be stimulated by inquiry itself, or by the conclusions of such inquiry. Sometimes it is advanced that no matter what universals or laws social science detects, human behavior will change either through natural evolution or conscious redirection, thus invalidating them. This point often leads to some confusing logical gamesmanship about how, and in what sequence of maneuvers, the researcher can outguess his phenomena. For example, it is sometimes asserted that behavioral reactions to social scientific inquiry can be built into hypotheses, thus rendering such reactions impotent to destroy validity.

This problem is not as formidable as it appears. There is often a confusion of the experimental level with that of the social system, or an assumption that the problems of the former level would automatically inhere in the latter. At the experimental level, preventing the artificial stimuli generated by the research itself from altering the natural action and interaction of phenomena in such a way as to thwart valid inquiry is a real problem. But it is not unique to social science. Careful experimental procedure and sound epistemology must seek to preclude such halo effects whether the research involves the psychologist's facial expression or the physicist's laser. Again, social scientists' perceptions of the nature of their task tend to be distorted by their failure to realize their goals. It is more difficult for them to deal with this problem at present. But it has not been convincingly demonstrated that this is an inherent phenomenological difference between social science and "hard science," rather than one of scientific capacity; or that the difference in scientific capacity is in turn a direct result of unique phenomenological problems of social science.

The basic problem facing political science involves the failure to recognize and deal with the goals and context of explanation. There have been two primary routes to such failure. The first looks to simplistic interpretations of "explanation" in the physical and natural sciences as the model to be emulated, and at times approaches chiliastic idolatry. Insufficient consideration is given to both how the interpretations fit with what *actually* happens in hard science and what consequences, beyond those assumed, their transplantation holds for political inquiry.[10] The interpretations of mainstream political science concerning the history of hard science and the role of those modes of explanation that have been borrowed from it are usually assumed to be self-evident if not unchallengeable. A passing acquaintance with the literature of the philosophy of science soon dispels such assumptions.[11]

The second route to failure tries to reject the strict transplantation of the explanatory style of hard science and to develop a style tailored to the exigencies of political science. The lack of success of such efforts stems from their inability to do more than free themselves from the straitjacket of the hypothetico-deductive style.[12] Escaping the rigidity or inappropriateness of this style of explanation is one matter; discovering a viable alternative is more difficult.[13]

In his landmark work, *The Political System* (1953), David Easton blames the discipline's low scientific capacity on the dominance of "hyperfactualism" and "reformism," which he views as precipitating a lack of attention to theoretical questions in research and methodology.[14] His analysis is aware of the political context of explanation: its potential relevance to public policy. It talks of the need for "realistic" knowledge in policy decisions and of the hazards of its absence. Yet, when Easton published his *Framework for Political Analysis* in 1965 to show what such theory might look like, the level of abstraction was still what C. Wright Mills terms "grand theory": a choice of focus so general that "practitioners cannot logically get down to observation." [15] The "framework" is contextually meaningless in terms of both substantive inquiry and the problems of viable explanation. In attempting to say nearly everything about both, it says little that is enlightening or useful about either.

This deficiency is characteristic of the manic-depressive approach to explanation that the profession manifests. In some instances, political scientists become so uncritically elated about the hypothetico-deductive model of "hard science" that all the problems of epistemology and the sociology of knowledge are assumed to be solved.[16] In other instances, they rebel against the rigidity and incongruity of the model by rejecting it in favor of ad hoc concoctions that fail to provide a way to discern when explanations are valid and when they are not.[17]

An important dimension of the context of explanation is the potential relevance of inquiry to the political process of the knowledgeable society. The logical character of explanation is a primary determinant of the actual and potential policy role of what is purported to be "knowledge." This must be a central concern in developing a mode of explanation. Determining in what manner we validly "explain" cannot be divorced from the public policy consequences of this determination or of the failure to make such a determination. This is not to say that all inquiry must serve policy goals or that it should serve certain values. It simply means that definitions of "explanation" and "knowledge" differ in their rigor and that such differences influence, to some degree, the latitude afforded institutions, elites, or individuals in using the "knowledge" that the profession generates. The more precisely defined and theoretically refined explanatory conclusions are, the less latitude there is for forging convincing ad hoc interpretations of their meaning. In this sense they are less susceptible to misinterpretations, or to manipulative uses designed to support or legitimize ideological positions.[18]

Toward Epistemic Craftsmanship: A Conception of Science

Before dealing with some of the specific problems of explanation, this analysis will elaborate a conception of the scientific enterprise as it pertains to political inquiry. The first point concerns the nature of scientific knowledge. Through pragmatic necessity dictated by the nature of its phenomena, political "science" should seek a functional rather than absolute kind of knowledge.

Hans Reichenbach is correct in asserting that the kind of knowledge sought is a major characteristic separating science from moral philosophy.[19] Science abjures the pursuit of universal moral directives and an absolute, teleological knowledge of causality in favor of a verifiable understanding of the world. Here, "functional" means useful, valid knowledge that is neither perfect (in the sense that all variables and relationships of causation are known) nor expressly moral in content. On the latter point, Reichenbach contends that the age-old dream of rationalist, moral philosophers was to discover ultimate and unchallengeable moral principles through reason; he rules this out of scientific endeavor by taking the position that the "ought" components of propositions can never be logically validated by science or garnered from it, and are therefore alien to the scientific enterprise.[20]

While recognizing the value consequences of "science" and the value biases that can attend its pursuit, this analysis agrees with Reichenbach that the search for universal moral truths is not a productive path to functional knowledge but, instead, a utopian perversion of scientific goals. Moreover, a science must not become fixated with an ultimate knowledge of causality to the extent that the development of functional knowledge suffers. Political science would waste its intellectual resources if it sought exclusively the ultimate causes of regime instability while neglecting the development of valid operational indices that could help predict and/or understand such instability—even in the absence of exact knowledge of causal sequences.

The definition of "functional knowledge" employed by political science must be even more flexible than that offered by Reichenbach and the more ardent logical positivists. Logical positivism and prescriptions for science that are analogous to it are often only slightly less rigid than the rational moralism from which they so intensely seek a total disassociation. At times, the extreme rigidity of logical positivism constitutes a secular mystique with an ontological and metaphysical faith in itself that contradicts its stated purpose. Reichenbach's *The Rise of Scientific Philosophy,* for example, is as much a strident philosophical opposition to the historical role of rationalist, moral philosophy as it is a treatise on scientific thinking. These intellectual currents are relevant to political science precisely because behavioralism represents the ascendency of an epistemological approach grounded in logical positivism and British empiricism.[21]

Two unfortunate inflexibilities in logical positivism, which are incongruous with the context of political inquiry, involve conceptions of validity and universal laws. With regard to validity, extreme logical positivism has little patience with probabilistic kinds of explanations. Its penchant for universal laws sometimes dictates an all-or-nothing notion of validity: after one or several contrary empirical instances, hypotheses may end up in the scrap heap. This kind of orientation has fostered within political science a conception of empirical validity that tends to be unbending and mechanical.[22] Hypothesis testing is often conceived as analogous to testing a light bulb: if it lights up, it is correct; if not, it is best discarded. While this approach does reflect a basic element of scientific consciousness, that one accepts or rejects hypotheses upon the basis of empirical evidence rather than upon mere preference or intuition, the simple and automatic view of acceptance or rejection has been dysfunctional. It has led to what Easton terms "hyperfactualism" and to simplistic induction and/or deduction that stake scientific endeavor too heavily upon the congruity of data and hypotheses, while neglecting the theoretical quality and scientific consciousness of hypotheses themselves.

To elaborate, political scientists have been led, consciously or unconsciously, by the logical positivist position to be more concerned with pushing out and testing hypotheses than with building hypotheses that are theoretically sound.[23] Logical positivism is mostly concerned with excluding moral philosophy, proving or disproving hypotheses, and welding proved hypotheses into universal laws or "constructional systems": panoplies of proved laws and hypotheses.[24] While these are an important and legitimate part of the scientific enterprise, the narrow fixation upon which activities and the overemphasis upon them that characterizes logical positivism has led many political scientists to an automatic view of science, the assumption and consequences of which are largely unknown to them. The view can be characterized as follows. In its inductive form, its exhortations call for the collection of data, and in great quantities.[25] Then it prescribes: develop from the data hypotheses that will make sense of the data. When the hypotheses are correct, they will "fit" the data. That is, they will be congruent with it and "explain" its patterned relationships. Fit successful hypotheses together and build laws or theories. In deductive form, the automatic view is even simpler. It prescribes developing a hypothesis, collecting data that seem relevant, and checking the congruence of data and hypothesis as a test of validity.

To the unwary, the automatic view may appear to capture the essence of scientific endeavor. The problem is that without careful attention to the theoretical quality, logical capacity, and phenomenological importance of both data and hypotheses, one can easily substitute sterile logical gamesmanship, pseudo-science, or "abstracted empiricism" for the pursuit of reliable knowledge.[26] Owing to its lack of broader theoretical and epistemic perspectives, the automatic view could amuse itself indefinitely by testing such barren or tautological hypotheses as "instability causes revolutions," or by discerning the patterned relationships among such data as telephone listings and weather forecasts.

Logical positivism's confining emphasis upon the pursuit of universal laws or systems of laws through experimental methods seems to have left the impression among many political scientists that there is little to contemplate about the nature and functions of "science." It is assumed that when one hits upon a "correct" hypothesis, it will be borne out by empiricism; when a sufficient number of hypotheses of sufficient scope are borne out, laws of political behavior will emerge. As Braybrooke and Rosenberg have noted: "Bahovioralist political scientists, in their eagerness to profit from useful precedents in the natural sciences, may have attached themselves too rigidly to the early doctrines of the positivist movement." [27]

It is improbable that the automatic view can produce a meaningful understanding of political phenomena. What is most needed is theoretically informed inquiry that will make sense of the dynamics of politics. Extreme or simplistic logical positivism cannot assure an escape from ignorance or myth. To hypothesize that the poor have less optimistic attitudes and a lower sense of political efficacy than those who are more economically satisfied is an hypothesis that can be substantiated by a vast quantity of data. To arrange a number of such "proved" hypotheses together into a law—"Political and economic attitudes vary among economic and political categories"—may be a logically precise activity, but few practitioners would be very sanguine about the comprehension that such "proved" hypotheses or laws could afford.

The negative influence of extreme or simplistic logical positivism upon political science has been to precipitate a confusion of the goals of scientific endeavor with its activities and methods. A functional knowledge and understanding demands scientific consciousness and epistemic craftsmanship. Compiling data, hypothesizing, and testing hypotheses are indispensable activities, but they are not the intrinsic goals of science; nor can they, by themselves, provide a realization of the goal of "understanding." Neither induction nor deduction is inherently fruitful, no matter how "objective," unless it is theoretically informed. This is because, as Norwood Russell Hanson observes, "causes certainly are connected with effects; but this is because our theories connect them, not because the world is held together by cosmic glue. The world *may* be glued together by imponderables, but that is irrelevant for causal explanation." [28]

The problem with extreme or simplistic logical positivism is that facts are assumed to have some existence, some inherency, beyond human cognition. Like atoms, which existed before they were seen, the facts of political life are assumed to be there, waiting for the magic bullet of a correct hypothesis to uncover them.

The pervasiveness of such views is due in part to the interpretation of the history of "hard science" that dominates political science, and that fosters what may be characterized as the "blind fisherman" approach to scientific progress. Casting with the fishpole of experimental method, the scientist patiently waits for the strike that will allow him to reel in the "facts." The absence of a broader theoretical consciousness and of epistemic craftsmanship blinds him to what is being pulled in—whether seaweed or bass—but he knows when something is on the line.

The embrace of extreme or simplistic logical positivism is also fostered by the respect and awe with which many social scientists perceive the achievements of their counterparts in the "hard sciences." But if one agrees with Hanson and Kuhn that perspectives of inquiry do not just find or miss "facts," but in a very real sense create them as viable cognitive entities, then the narrow experimental methods of relating hypotheses to data and vice versa are dependent upon the scientific consciousness of the perspective that spawns hypothesization and data accretion so far as functional knowledge is concerned.[29] As logical positivism dictates, we need empirical validation, but this is not synonymous with "understanding." Though the automatic view of science is "functional" in contrast to rational moral philosophy, it is not "functional" enough for political science. The complexity of political phenomena does not preclude valid, scientific knowledge, but it does preclude attaining a meaningful understanding through exclusive reliance or heavy emphasis upon automatic conceptions of science. What is needed is epistemic craftsmanship that guides the precision, theoretical quality, and utility of hypothesization. The goal of "understanding" and the procdures and concepts of epistemology that demonstrably separate that "understanding" from ideology and ignorance must bring hypothesization out of the sterile abyss of automatic science.

The conception of science described here seeks to exclude the unproductive and often self-deceiving extremes of "grand theory" and "abstracted empiricism."[30] "Grand theory" leaps to what it hopes are deductive principles, but becomes so abstract and nebulous that empirical verification is impossible. Abstracted empiricism becomes so enamored with verification that "the dogmatic requirement for such verification often seems the sole concern, and hence limits or even determines the concepts used and the problems taken up by those committed to this microscopic style." [31] Such is the intellectual poverty of extreme methodism, simplistic experimental science, or excessively abstract deductivism.

Epistemic craftsmanship demands that flexibility be an integral part of the scientific conception. Flexibility does not mean ad hoc science; pseudo-science, but that there are different ways of pursuing valid knowledge. Depending upon the scientific capacity of a discipline, the context of its inquiries, and the nature of its focus, it may validly and productively opt for different approaches to "science" at different times. Epistemic craftsmanship seeks to use every logical and empirical weapon at hand to assure that the approach employed is justified in scientifically conscious terms so that flexibility does not become a carte blanche for self-deception and quackery. To assure this, a field of scientific inquiry must justify the congruence between its approach to science and its stage of scientific devlopment not only pragmatically, but epistemically as well.

Illustratively, for a social science discipline in an embryonic state of scientific development where established axioms, theories, and operational constructs are largely absent, it is both pragmatic and epistemically justifiable to concentrate upon defining the problems to be solved and upon delineating the nature of the phenomena studied. To do so, heavy emphasis might be placed upon model-building, developing classificatory schemata and taxonomic systems, and producing descriptive, monographic materials. A major goal of epistemic craftsmanship is to keep such activities in their logical place: to discourage the illusion that they constitute the causal explanations that science seeks.[32]

Eugene Meehan draws a distinction between "theory" and "quasi-theory." The latter comprises models, analogies, and taxonomic systems that categorize, speculate, and conceptualize, but that cannot logically explain in an empirically verifiable manner.[33] Quasi--theory possesses no self-contained epistemic mechanisms by which one could validate, or invalidate its conclusions. It may offer no hypotheses at all. If it does, it does not render them vulnerable to repudiation on other than an intuitive, extra-scientific basis. Real theory offers an explicit and integrated conceptual framework that causally explains (in the sense of functional rather than absolute knowledge) the action and interaction of phenomena in a manner potentially subject to empirical verification or repudiation.

Quasi-theoretical devices are epistemically proper for organizing perceptions of phenomena, finding patterns among variables, and getting a feeling for which "facts" we need to know. But to confuse valuable heuristics with causal explanations or with the activities of mature science is to lose heuristic value altogether. Such confusion leads political science too quickly from the cautious exploration of its phenomena without providing any effective means for concluding whether the leap from description to causal explanation is anything but fantasy.

Only epistemic craftsmanship can render flexibility a boon to the pursuit of valid knowledge. "Flexibility" means not assuming that any single approach to science will always serve optimally, regardless of the state of its knowledge and scientific progress. Nor can it be *assumed* that some previously developed concept of "flexibility" will suffice. For example, F. S. C. Northrop offers a multi-stage schema of scientific evolution,[34] while asserting that the problems faced by a "science" should determine the methods used. The first stage involves the initiation of inquiry and the analysis of problems. Both Baconian induction and deductively formulated theory are, according to Northrop, inappropriate and premature in this stage. Stage one ends only when it is known what facts must be discovered in order to resolve the problems that initiated inquiry. At stage two, Baconian induction is employed to inspect the facts designated in stage one. Finally, deductive theory becomes appropriate. Northrop's schema may be relevant and helpful to the scientifically conscious pursuit of political knowledge, but if it is, it must be convincingly demonstrated to be so in terms of the substance and context of political science and the state of its epistemic progress. It cannot merely be legislated into the profession, or the virtues of both flexibility and epistemic craftsmanship are lost.

Epistemic craftsmanship involves questioning each existing approach and method within a science not from an anti-scientific perspective, but from a functional and analytical one:

a. What epistemic or theoretical functions does it now perform?

b. What are its assumed or proposed functions in the collective perception of the scientific discipline?

c. What, if any, incongruities exist between a and b?

d. What are the epistemic and theoretical assets and liabilities of this approach or method, considering a, b, and c; and considering the problems, context, and goals of inquiry?

For example, many social scientists view the null hypothesis as a device that is as appropriate and indispensable to social science as the telescope is to astronomy. This may be true, but it must be demonstrated and constantly checked. If it is simply accepted, social science may not be aware when it is no longer so. It is often assumed that the viability and appropriateness of the null hypothesis in social science rests on the complexity and behavioristic nature of the phenomena studied, in contrast to hard science. Such an assumption—that the device is somehow inherently rooted in the phenomena studied—all but precludes the necessity of the type of evaluation and reevaluation that is so central to epistemic craftsmanship. Moreover, there is little reason to accept the assumption.

As previously stated, social scientists tend to attribute the dearth of their epistemic progress to the complexity of their phenomena. Ignorance is credited more to the nature of the universe, or to the phenomenological lot of such disciplines than to a lack of epistemic progress. The difference is all-important. Blaming the phenomena leads to a fatalistic view and is conducive to making the best of what little we have until something big breaks for us, and political science suddenly fully approximates physics or biology. In this view, epistemic craftsmanship is usually conceived as being synonymous with the explanatory millennium; more specifically, with an established "science of politics." Wallowing in scientific self-pity, the view comes close to protestation that there is little or nothing that can be done until scientific problems are solved.

With regard to the null hypothesis, Charles E. Woodson indicates that the reason psychology employs it and physics does not is not that the disciplines differ inherently, but, rather, that physics is more advanced in its epistemology." [35] He contends that the physicist *could* use the null hypothesis, but chooses the method of parameter estimation instead because his theoretical constructs and techniques of measurement are superior to those used in psychology. Moreover, the need to evaluate the choice of approaches and methods through epistemic craftsmanship is given substantive illustration by an interesting methodological paradox involving physics and psychology.[36] Paul E. Meehl states that "because physical theories typically predict numerical values, an improvement in experimental precision reduces the tolerance range and hence increases corroborability. In most psychological research, improved power of a statistical design leads to a prior probability approaching ½ of finding a significant difference in the theoretically predicted direction. Hence the corroboration yielded by 'success' is very weak and becomes weaker with increased precision." Meehl concludes: " 'Statistical significance' plays a logical role in psychology precisely the reverse of its role in physics."

In political science, as well as in social science generally, there is a compelling need for the kind of introspection described as epistemic craftsmanship.

PART II: THE LOGICAL COMPONENTS OF EXPLANATION IN POLITICAL INQUIRY

This part attempts to resolve some confusions in the epistemological literature by examining the mechanics of viable explanation in political inquiry. The logical requisites for explanation offered here are tentative, and are not purported to constitute "the way" of explanation or the arrival of a scientific millenium. The purpose is not to saddle political inquiry with a particular set of rigid explanatory concepts, but, rather, to present a discussion of the parameters of explanation: a discussion conducive to the kind of epistemic craftsmanship that is the core of intellectual progress.

In any discipline, the question "How do we know what we claim to know?" is to an important degree answered by a definition for "explanation." The one offered here is not a relativist one. The basic assumption is that there is more to valid explanation than the context in which it exists; that there exist processes of thought that are central to explanation and that have a consequence beyond its substance and context. Without such an assumption, explanation cannot be dealt with in any meaningful, generic sense.

This analysis does not contend that explanation is the only proper activity of science in all of its stages of development. An embryonic "science" may legitimately spend much of its time and energy finding out what it needs to know. But a viable concept of explanation, while not synonymous with 'the pursuit of science, must be present. It must be available to perform when the profession is ready to fruitfully employ it.

If that which political science claims to know is to be scientifically valid (and thus distinguishable from conventional wisdom and ideology), then the profession must manifest an epistemically viable concept of explanation in order to render it so. It is often charged (and deservedly so) by critics of certain explanatory models that equating science and explanation is too rigid.[1] But this does not mean that authentic science can do without a definition of explanation. If political scientists, armed with a concept of explanation, prematurely attempt to "explain"—while neglecting the preparatory work of analyzing phenomena and discovering which facts must be "known"—then the concept of explanation is misused, and both science and understanding are impeded. If, however, there is no sufficiently developed concept of explanation to call upon (and explanation comes to mean any substantive discussion that sounds convincing), then inquiry is in very fundamental difficulty.

Professor John Gunnell is correct in his contention that "Explanation (or intelligibility) is not merely a psychological matter, for what will count as explanation as well as what requires explanation is pragmaticlly determined against a framework of ideas about reality, theories, and rules which together constitute a paradigm or conceptual scheme for interpreting or organizing experience."[2] But such pragmatism must refer only to the context of particular explanations, not to the contextualism of "explanation" as a logical process. Goals for understanding and the context of political inquiry are both relevant to explanations: to their pursuit, use, and consequence. This does not preclude the establishment of generic, logical characteristics for explanation as a process.

Without such characteristics, politicians and political scientists would be indistinguishable in terms of epistemic reliability of their vocational endeavors. Both desire to "explain," and, moreover, to make those "explanations" contextually relevant. Political scientists cannot trust politicians to weave their desires and contextual insights into reliable knowledge of political reality, for the same reasons that political scientists cannot trust themselves to do the same—in the absence of an independent standard of explanation to assess what purports to be political knowledge. The context and goals of explanations should inform modes and processes of explanation. They should not, however, hold such modes and processes prisoners of the biases described by the sociology of knowledge.[3]

There are too many definitions of "explanation." Too often, there is a confusion of kinds of explanations with the process of explanation. Because this process cannot be totally context bound and still produce valid, reliable knowledge, various methods of explanation must meet similar criteria of validity.

In *Explanation in Social Science,* Robert Brown depicts seven "common methods" of social "explanation" that "bear directly upon the work of social scientists": genetic, intentions, dispositions, reasons, functions, empirical generalizations, and theories.[4] Brown's typology presents myriad levels and processes of inquiry, resulting in a confused tratment of epistemic issues. By treating explanation in terms of its substance or style (rather than its logic), Brown is merely traveling a more subtle route to contextualism, while attempting to preserve the trappings of science. In epistemic terms, Brown's typology furnishes no justification for including or excluding anything offered as "explanation." Because logical derivation and empirical validity are not the defining characteristics, divine revelation has as much claim to inclusion as the seven modes selected.

The fate of the scientific enterprise at the hands of such arbitrary and barren treatments of "explanation" is vividly clear from Brown's exposition: "The importance of intention-explanations in daily life does not seem open to serious doubt. We explain why Ruth kicked her husband's foot under the dining table by saying that her 'intention'—or 'desire' or 'wish'—was to have him be quiet. . . ." [5] This constitutes description, not explanation.

Unless a definition of explanation includes some standards for validity, its function becomes analogous to "natural law" arguments. That is, arguing that one's moral viewpoint is superior or correct because it is in some sense not merely an opinion but a natural law is analogous to stating that an empirical contention is superior or correct because it constitutes an "explanation." In both cases, the logical poverty of the appeals renders the terms devices of debate: inflated and solely emotive glorifications of the position argued or conclusions reached. "Common sense" definitions of the process of explanation have no connection with valid science, except to debase it to pseudo-science.[6]

This does not imply that explanation is synonymous with absolute or certain knowledge. As Mills puts it: "Of course, it is true that we are never certain; in fact, that we are often 'guessing,' but it is not true that all guesses have an equal chance of being correct." [7]

Contextual definitions of explanation (such as Brown's), and/or the neglect of the logic of explanation in favor of its descriptive substance, grants all "guesses" a kind of parity. Such epistemological egalitarianism is neither logically justifiable nor pragmatic.

If political science were searching for a productive approach to studying the psychic motivations of elite behavior, and if it were confronted with two "explanations," one offered by a manual laborer who posited that "all politicians are nuts," and another offered by Harold Lasswell that deeply rooted pathological tendencies are politically salient, the discipline would (for reason of professional solidarity alone) embrace Lasswell's explanation. But what of the more difficult choices among equally plausible and articulate "explanations" that cannot be sharply differentiated according to the reputation of the scholars who offer them? Without some standards for the logic of explanation, the researcher or theorist can only trust that intuition or luck is on his side. However, some explanations *can* be demonstrated to better than others in terms of their logical derivation and the reliability of their conclusions. Authentic science is demarcated through such rigor. It is "reliability" that distinguishes valid, functional explanation from myth and speculation.

The Reliability of Explanation

The conception of reliability offered here is extremely important to the context of inquiry and the pursuit of knowledge. Reliability is required for valid explanation, theory, and knowledge. Before stating why it is all three, it is necessary to elaborate the meaning of reliability in all three contexts.

Reliability does not mean empirical certainty. It is not purported that the pursuit of reliability will necessarily produce a full-blown science of politics. Nor does the concept of reliability constitute a veiled plea for isolation from public policy problems via "ivory tower" scholarship. Rather, reliability requires that a logically sound epistemic basis for conclusions is manifested. That is, that clear links with empirical reality and a dependence upon it exist and are demonstrated. This capacity to link arguments and conclusions with empirical reality and to render them dependent upon it through explicit and testable constructs is basic to notions of "contingency" and "falsification."

"Contingency," as described by George C. Homans, refers to the ability of an explanation to render itself dependent upon changes in empirical reality. When contingency is manifested, one can observe (in a meaningful and conclusive way) how those alterations in phenomena that are crucial to the theoretical, explanatory, or hypothetical offering in question actually bear upon the validity or reliability of that offering.[8] Contingency, therefore, requires a linking of theoretical and observational terms. The theory itself constitutes only a formal model of relationships among abstract theoretical concepts. Its empirical relevance must be created through the gradual development of supplementary generalizations, procedures, and assumptions. These specify what domain of observation statements is to be deemed relevant to the theoretical statements, and what range of values for the observational quantities will be taken as confirming theoretical predictions.[9] Without such a capacity to be contingent, an offering must be judged in extra-scientific terms only. Without testable links to the phenomena explained, there are no valid means for determining if the "explanation" is reliable or not.

Karl Popper's notion of "falsification" adds an important element to the idea of contingency.[10] Many varieties of the relativist position argue that "truth" and "proof" are derived exclusively from subjective perception.[11] "Proving them to whom?" is a legitimate question. However, because we can still find persons who insist that the world is flat, should we abandon geography, astronomy, and physics? The point is that there are still gains to be made in intellectual progress and scientifically competent knowledge even if "proofs" are in no way total or certain. Popper's insight is that the kind of reliability just described is exceedingly important even if it cannot produce absolute proof of what is offered, for it can still provide for its falsification.

Nevertheless, falsification cannot be defined in such a strict manner as to treat a single counterinstance to a theory as requiring the theory's rejection. While in logical terms a universal statement is indeed invalidated by a single counterinstance, in scientific practice theories only *treat* their component relations as invariant. When a theory is operationalized, exceptions always occur. It is therefore necessary to permit the treatment of at least some counterinstances as exceptions, or potential falsifiers, rather than as actual falsifiers. Limiting conventions and the manner of operationalization serves to restrict "universal" theories to phenomenological areas where they are valid empirically.[12]

Reliability, then, is the capacity to provide for a test of what is purported to be the contribution of the theory, explanation, or hypothesis (contingency), and then require that the explanation under consideration actually meet this test to an adequate degree (successful subjection to falsification).[13] Through contingency and falsification, reliability provides a standard for assessing the relationship between a theory and its context, *a standard that is independent of any particular context*. While explanations differ in their degree of reliability, what is required is that reliability be maximized wherever possible, both in the construction of particular explanations and in the choice among alternative ones.

Reliability is not just one quality of valid explanation, nor is it *primus inter pares*. It is *the* essential quality without which science, explanation, and valid knowledge cannot exist. All other characteristics of explanation, including its phenomenological scope, range of predictive power, and contribution to man's ability to control his world, not only depend upon reliability, but can be judged only in relation to it.[14] What other logical basis is there for accepting a theory? Surely we cannot be sanguine about its utility or scientific quality merely because it subsumes large portions of political reality. The questions: How good is it? What is it worth? What does it tell us? can be answered only in terms of reliability. Without it, there is no quality at all, in the scientific sense. Without a determination of reliability, one may evaluate the style, ideology, or ambition of the endeavor, but never its contribution to science or knowledge—if "evaluation" means more than normative preference or intuition.

Once the reliability of an explanation has been successfully established, it should *then* be assessed according to other criteria. These are of two sorts. First, there are standards of theory construction that are not subsumed under the concept of reliability, because they do not deal directly with the relationship between empirical and theoretical terms, as do contingency and falsification. For example, Abraham Kaplan's "norm of coherence" stipulates that an explanation should be constructed in as simple a manner as is possible, and that it should normally be congruent with previously established theories.[15] Coherence in both of these senses represents an assessment of the relationship between different theoretical terms. Observational entities are not part of this comparison, which must therefore be made only with theories that have previously demonstrated their empirical stature.

Second, reliable explanations may be assessed in normative terms, by the degree to which they deal with problems and phenomena in which we are really interested. If the predictions and conclusions of explanation fail to address such concerns, or explanatory premises appear to conflict with preferred values, then it is legitimate to reconsider the explanation. However, unless such reconsideration leads to the construction of an alternative explanation of at least equal reliability with the first, it is not legitimate to *reject* the former on normative grounds. Any such rejection would constitute an intrusion of values into the process of falsification. Stated in positive terms, preferred values may serve as the premises of inquiry, insofar as reliable explanations can be generated from them.

The requirement of reliability applies equally to hypothesization, theorization, and explanation. While these may involve different levels of inquiry and have a different scope, predictive power, utility, and semantic construction, each must meet the same standard, or be treated as possessing, at most, heuristic value. This postulation of a common goal for all forms and levels of understanding is close to Popper's conception of "unity of method." That is, whether in the natural sciences or the social (and whether the activity be explanation, prediction, or testing), there is no great difference in logical structure.[16] While Popper's trinity of method includes prediction and testing, and the one presented here refers to hypothesization and theorization, the two are essentially similar. Testing is necessary to the reliability of explanations, theories, and hypotheses. Prediction is also necessary to the reliability of all three; but this is a logical necessity and not because prediction is the inherent goal.

Prediction

Prediction, and its role in explanation, have been a matter of much confusion in social science. There also exists in the philosophy of science a heated debate concerning the symmetry of prediction and explanation.[17] N. R. Hanson asserts that the two are different because one can "predict" without "explaining." Ptolemy, Hanson argues, had great success predicting astronomical movements, but could not correctly explain them because he pictured the earth as the center of our galaxy.[18] It is true that one can predict without explaining: without knowing the causal sequences and the "why" of predicted events. This analysis follows Popper in holding that the above difference is not one of formal logic, but, rather, one of substantive goal or result.[19]

The formal aspects of logic and epistemology are, for all practical purposes, the same, whether one wants to predict or to explain. Both goals rest upon reliability. If this is present, then the theory, hypothesis, or explanation in question may have as its function prediction, explanation, or both.

It is sometimes charged that the "prediction-generalization" model of inquiry is an unproductive approach for political science. The genuine complaint is that the scope and/or level of prediction or generalization sought tend to be much too grandiose to be productive.[20] This fault results from the manner in which these attempts have been executed, and not the logical processes of prediction and generalization themselves. If pursuing the goal of "predicting" has not been fruitful, it is not because prediction is dysfunctional or dispensable, but, rather, because particular predictions have been unreliable. For example, Thomas L. Thorson argues that the deficiencies of Easton's major conceptual works are precipitated by his fixation for the "prediction-generalization" model.[21] It is not the model that leads Easton to an often unproductive level of abstraction. This results instead from his failure to recognize and employ prediction as an integral part of falsification, while at the same time holding it to be a primary goal of science.

Prediction and explanation are not identical in all respects. One can successfully predict rain in his local environment from observations of immediate weather patterns, with the help of accumulated experimental clues concerning clouds and air moisture. This can be done with no ability to causally explain the sequence of meteorological events that actually produces rain. On the other hand, one could explain rain as the condensation of moisture on dust particles in the atmosphere (and test this in the controlled environment of laboratory experimentation) without ever possessing the observational skills and experiential clues needed to leave the laboratory, go outside, and predict rain. There are two roles for prediction: as a logical process, and as a goal.

Whether one seeks to explain or to predict is, as Popper contends, a pragmatic determination.[22] If one is a student of physics, the laboratory condensation experiment may be adequate, because the purpose may be that of explaining the meteorological sequences that cause rain. If, in contrast, one is a Connecticut Valley tobacco farmer, prediction will be very useful even in the absence of the physicist's explanation. This pragmatic choice of whether prediction or explanation will best serve our needs must not be confused with prediction's functioning as a logical part of explanation. Whether one seeks to predict the incidence of rain or to explain its causal sequence in meteorological terms, "prediction" as a logical device is indispensable. It is true by definition that, in order to predict as a goal, one must go through some process of logic whose result is a "prediction." But what of explanation?

Explanation, too, needs the logical process of prediction, but it does not need the goal of prediction. That is, it requires predictions of a theoretical or experimental type that may or may not serve to predict in the pragmatic sense. Explanations may involve predictions of a sort that have no pragmatic use in predicting those aspects of phenomena that we would like to predict. To predict that condensation upon dust particles produces precipitation is, in the logical sense, as much a correct prediction as looking out over a stormy sky and predicting rain. But only in the logical sense; not the pragmatic sense.

Prediction in the logical sense is necessary for valid explanation precisely because reliability too is essential. Without predictions of the logical type, no contingency or falsification is possible. In order for explanation to be contingent upon changes in observed phenomena, such changes must be predicted. Likewise, an explanation cannot be either subjected to falsification or falsified unless it is possible to deduce and operationalize predictions of observed events. The logic of explanation and prediction are thus similar. For this reason, it is not possible either to conclusively validate or to repudiate a theory, hypothesis, or explanation that lacks predictive power; at least not in any authentically scientific sense. An explanation may fail to predict what we want to know, but it cannot fail to predict in the logical sense.

This analysis has asserted that scientific explanation is not synonymous with common sense, and cannot be so. Common sense and conventional wisdom may produce pragmatic prediction, but they do not contain the predictive logic of explanation. They can tell *what* will happen, but not *why*. Political science faces a phenomenological focus that precludes the attainment of a broad and competent understanding through common sense. Only at very simplistic levels can we predict directly from observed phenomena without explaining them, and still avoid circular reasoning. We can predict the percentage of votes a candidate will receive without knowing exactly why—except that a certain number of people voted for him. However, in order to pragmatically predict most of the important and complex aspects of political life, some logical predictive power is required.

Political scientists will not, for example, be able to predict the political instability of regimes (beyond the tautological level of asserting that instability will occur when conditions become unstable), unless they can predict (in the logical sense) what those conditions are: predict the *why* of instability. This does not mean that we must have absolute knowledge of casual sequences, but that political instability will demand more of the logical kind of prediction before we can either predict in the pragmatic sense or explain. Unlike rain, political instability is not a clear-cut phenomenon providing very obvious clues that sustain accurate prediction in the pragmatic sense.

Logical or explantory prediction can become the theoretical basis for longer-range predictions that are more anticipatory and of greater use. Because the tobacco farmer's pragmatic prediction lacks the intricate, theoretically informed predictive power of the physicist's explanation, the farmer is limited to a local and observational kind of prediction. The explanatory prediction of the physicist's experiments can eventually provide the kind of knowledge that will be of even more pragmatic utility than the farmer's nonexplanatory predictions. It can be used to establish a higher plane of observation and prediction not confined to a local area and not dependent upon what can be seen directly overhead. Such is the progress of real science, where the explanatory type of prediction can supersede or enhance nonexplanatory, pragmatic predictions.

Generalization

The role of generalization in explanation has been obsecured by a confusion of the scope of explanation with its validity. Perceiving that much of the "theoretical" literature of political science is in the realm of "grand theory" and that the emphasis of such nebulous endeavors is on generalization, Thorson names "generalization" itself (along with prediction) as the villain.[23] A fixation for generalization (probably related to the dominance of logical positivist models and their penchant for universal laws) can be premature, rigid, and unproductive if divorced from scientific consciousness—and from a knowledge of what we need to know. Although often attempted, a grand level or broad scope of generalization is not necessary for explanation. Generalization as a logical process—defined as the escape from contextualism or relativism through applying explanations to more than a single instance—*is* required both for prediction and reliability. Prediction operates by means of generalization: postulating that a certain defined type of event is always (or usually) the result of a set of causal antecedents. The concepts used in prediction (and explanation) themselves constitute a form of generalization: identifying "common" characteristics of "similar" events.[24] While no particular level or scope of generalization is required, it is necessary that explanation demonstrably apply to more than one situation, or it is merely a description that explains nothing.

The complexity of political phenomena renders generalization difficult, or presently impossible, at the scope and level at which we desire to know about politics. As a result, explanations may be "partial" or "incomplete" with regard to the relationship between the scope at which explanation can now be generalized and the scope at which we desire to understand. The terms "partial" and "incomplete" cannot signify the absence of generalization as a logical component of explanation, but only the lack of sufficient generalization for pragmatic explanation. Though some degree of generalization is necessary, the escape it provides from mere description and relativism may be exceedingly modest. Therefore, all explanations are not equally useful in the pragmatic sense. The logical reliability of generalization determines whether it possesses utility. If it does, the degree of utility is then affected by the level and scope of the generalization.

Deduction

The definition and role of deduction is an unresolved issue in social scientific inquiry. Opponents of deduction often equate it with syllogistic exercises in formal logic. In political science, its critics claim that the discipline's focus is too complex to sustain the effective use of deductive models.[25] This assessment confuses the dearth of epistemic progress with the complexity of its subject matter. If (as Kuhn and Hanson contend) both factual and theoretical concepts are created by perspectives of inquiry, then lack of scientific porgress requires reconceptualization, not resignation.[26] Perceived reality necessarily seems bewildering until it is explained, but this does not mean that deductive models of explanation are, *ipso facto,* inappropriate for such explanations simply because they cannot be immediately applied. While it is impossible to prove that every event can be deductively explained by a reliable theory, this is not sufficient reason to abandon the attempt to do so; nor, more importantly, does it deny the logical means to do so.[27] Any given event can always be "deduced," in the sense that a set of general and singular statements, or premises, from which it logically follows, can always be constructed. Such deduction constitutes explanation only if the criteria of reliability are met, but reliability can be determined only empirically. Therefore, it cannot be argued (or demonstrated) *logically* that any event cannot be reliably deduced.

Deduction thus provides at least a potential approach to explanation in any field of inquiry. In political science, the debate over its proper role cannot be enlightening until participants stop talking at cross purposes.[28] The major confusion, often resulting in armies of straw men, is between the necessity of deduction as a mental process (logical deduction from empirical premises) and deduction narrowly defined: either as syllogistic reasoning from certain premises to equally absolute (but empirically sterile) conclusions, or as the belief that the model of formal hypothetico-deductive theory adopted from the established sciences is, in itself, sufficient for the development of valid explanations.

Because prediction, generalization, and reliability are necessary for explanation, deduction too is required.[29] Not necessarily in the form of the deductive models of "hard science," and certainly not in the form of syllogistic constructs, but deduction as a mental process *is* necessary. Several cognitive confusions have impeded recognition of this necessity.

All successful explanations appear rigid and syllogistic by virtue of their success. Explanations must be generalizable beyond a single context, must predict something (however limited or useless), and must be demonstrated to be reliable through tests that show them to be contingent but do not result in their falsification. Because a successful explanation has gone through all this, it necessarily seems syllogistic and rigid. That is, its conclusions logically follow from its propositions and theoretical relationships. As Norton Long points out, this entails "a patterning of variables and their logical relationships, such that given the stated interactional rules, the phenomenon to be explained would logically result when the variables were given assigned values. The phenomenon in the explanation is logically entailed. This is the sense in which we predict, and the only sense in which we can do so with logical warrant. It is in no sense different from the schoolboy's algebra for calculating the progress of a boat on a stream. The logic applies to the relations in the formula." [30] Formulistic? Yes. Rigid? Yes, but only in retrospect.

The confusion lies in equating the *results* of successful explanation with its source. A successful explanation is rigidly deductive, but the development of that explanation is a matter of careful trial and error, not the instant application of some model as rigid as the final, successful product itself. A completed skyscrapper appears rigid and monolithic precisely because, like a successful explanation, it is a finished product. No competent architect would suggest that the way to build a skyscraper is to start with four solid pieces of prefabricated steel fifty stories in length; raise them up; connect them; slap on a single fifty-story piece of wall to each side; and then go inside and build the floors. This would be as unproductive and frustrating as taking the form of a successful explanation and "applying" it to the problems in which one is interested, but that have not previously been explained.

The successful product of science, a reliable explanation, does not become the instant solution to all the epistemic and phenomenological problems of a scientific community. Explanations are not like livestock that can be bred into a herd. Successful explanations do provide knowledge that helps us to craft other explanations. They do provide us with a model to aim at in order to successfully explain. But they do not, by themselves, manifest all of the scientific endeavor necessary for further explanations. If they did do so, then the first reliable explanation would constitute the scientific millennium.

Such misconceptions have obscured the fact that while deductive models or syllogisms cannot solve all of the problems of science, science cannot exist without deduction as a mental process. The latter, unlike syllogistic deduction, is not synonymous with certain knowledge, or even with the pursuit of universal empirical laws. May Brodbeck states: "The inadequacies of 'imperfect' knowledge do not affect the possibility of deduction." [31] Some general premise is required for pursuit and attainment of explanation, even though that premise need not be a natural law. [32] "Imperfect knowledge" is functional: it is "true" only relative to specified premises. The premises themselves, and therefore the conclusions, are tentative rather than absolute. Functional knowledge is incompatible with syllogistic deduction, but not with deduction as a mental process.

The role of deduction is not limited to its axiomatic posture in the final product (successful explanation). As Popper asserts: "I do not believe that we ever make inductive generalizations in the sense that we start with observations and try to derive our theories for them. I believe that the prejudice that we proceed in this way is a kind of scientific optical illusion, and that at no stage of scientific development do we begin without something in the nature of a theory, such as a hypothesis, or a prejudice, or a problem—often a technological one— which in some way guides our observations, and helps us to select from innumerable objects of observations those which may be of interest." [33]

The cumulative, incremental view of scientific history, coupled with reactions against the narrow rigidity of syllogistic models of explanation, has obscured the importance of deduction as a mental process. Not only is the latter manifested in successful explanation, but it is, at some stage, a prerequisite for that success. [34]

Whether one calls his endeavor induction or deduction, some generalizable, predictive, testable entity (whether a hypothesis or a theory, and regardless of its scope) must be arrived at—if explanation is to follow. It matters little whether this arrival is precipitated by "straight" induction from the data, "induction" that was really guided by an implicit theory or framework, "armchair" deduction divorced from direct empiricism, or by abduction, retrodiction, imagination, or delusion. [35] The origin of explanatory premises is of no major consequence, for the success or failure of the explanation is determined by the reliability of its deduced conclusions, and not its intellectual pedigree.

Induction makes a contribution to explanation only if it succeeds in producing a generalizable, predictive, testable construct, which is—by any definition—a deductive construct. Induction is dispensable if one can produce by some other means a deductive construct that is reliable.   Neither induction nor deduction is useful inherently or in isolation. Both may produce intellectually sterile approaches: abstracted empiricism or grand theory,[36] but this must not lead to the erroneous assumption that deduction is dispensable.

Causality

The concept of causality embraced here is a functional one. That is, if we discover and validly demonstrate that a certain variable has an independent rather than dependent status in producing some patterned relationships, and that it serves as a guidepost for prediction and generalization, then it will be taken as causal.   Though political scientists may find it difficult (and perhaps impossible) to discover even every proximal causal variable attending political phenomena, the kind of understanding sought excludes merely associating certain conditions with other conditions.   For this reason, the pursuit of functional, causal knowledge is necessary.   The pursuit of functional knowledge is a pragmatic choice grounded in the context and nature of political inquiry.

The characteristics that this analysis has ascribed to explanation render a functional concept of causality a necessary part of scientific inquiry.   Arthur S. Goldberg describes this necessity in substantive terms: "That correlation has been found to exist between self-identification, in terms of social class, and party identification, and that such correlation has been found in numerous studies, suggesting a general relationship between these two phenomena is, to me, no explanation whatever. Is is, instead, the stimulus for the question, 'Why does such a relationship exist?' An answer might be derived from an appropriate set of premises, and they, in turn, might be tested against the empirical aspects of their implications." [37]

Causality, therefore, is derived from the reliability of explanation, and constitutes a legitimate and necessary goal of inquiry.

Conclusion

The logical interrelationship of the previously described components of explanation is as follows:

Successful subjection to falsification is a necessary condition for reliability.

Contingency (by means of prediction) is a necessary condition for the successful subjection of an explanation to falsification.

Deduction from a set of premises is a necessary condition for the contingency of statements (including causal statements) concerning the phenomena for which explanation is sought.

These logical characteristics represent necessary conditions for viable explanation. They are also prerequisites for "coherence," "congruence," "simplicity," and similar other qualities of explanation.

Progress toward authentically scientific modes of inquiry and toward a comprehensive understanding requires that political science effectively come to terms with epistemological problems. The behavioral revolution has produced a more theoretical orientation, enhanced rigor, and yielded impressive aggregations of useful data, but underlying conceptions of epistemology upon which the quality of knowledge depends are too often neglected or assumed as given. This analysis (or any other dealing with the logic of explanation) cannot by itself advance our understanding of phenomena. Epistemological guidance for the modes and methods of inquiry must exist *within* the profession, rather than seeking to supersede or transcend it. It is only the criteria for valid explanation that must be independent of substance and context, certainly not the explanations themselves. Rather, the components of valid explanation posited here seek to require that the relationships between explanations and their contexts be logically established.

In order to be effective, the development of epistemological criteria must be linked directly to research and theory—in an operational sense. The status of the philosophy of science as an esoteric and often irrelevant field divorced from the profession's mainstream scholarship is a problem to be overcome, not a natural order or an immutable fact of intellectual life. It is not necessary that every working political scientist suspend research and theory-building until he or the profession arrives at the epistemological millennium. But neither is it prudent to treat scientific philosophy as an intellectual talisman whose symbolic presence can elevate the prestige (if not the validity) of inquiry.

The preceding analysis has attempted to illuminate the kinds of issues that are crucial to the attainment of scientific knowledge. If any or all of the logical components offered here *are* genuinely essential to explanation, even without constituting the complete set of sufficient conditions for competent explanation, then it is only by virtue of substantive research, theory-building, and epistemic craftsmanship that such claims can be demonstrated. It is not the particular issues raised here or the positions taken on them that constitute the epistemological imperative for political science. It is instead the necessity of a viable and productive answer to the question "How do we know what we claim to know?"

Some Problems of Values, Knowledge and Professional Dynamics

Previous discussions of biases in inquiry, the nature of knowledge and science, and the professional process provide useful perspectives for analyzing some of the problems and issues of contemporary political science. This chapter will examine the nature and interrelationships of: the professional repute system, definitions of "knowledge," value consequences of inquiry, and problems concerning claims of epistemic capacity.

Repute is basic to professionalism. Externally, an occupational group must command a minimum of lay deference in order to claim professional status. What separates a profession from a mere occupational category is its claim to be expert in its "service" area, and the perception by clients and the public of the legitimacy of that claim. What allows a political scientist to call himself a "professional" is that he is perceived to possess knowledge, techniques of inquiry, and certificates of achievement and training that separate him in the public mind from political publicists or secondary school civics teachers.

Internally, repute is for all professions both the primary means and primary substance of individual occupational status. It is also the principal mechanism by which the occupational peer group distributes rewards and sanctions. Furthermore, repute is the core of the professional process: providing models and contrast models of professional socialization and giving flesh to definitions of proper role and conduct, thereby shaping the substance of professional culture. Though the ideal functions of repute may be derived from organizational theory applied to the profession, its substantive influences in a given context are largely determined by its nature and sources.

The Somit and Tanenhaus study documented the scope and intensity of the profession's repute system as perceived by political scientists. The most significant finding for present purposes was that attributes contributing to career success were, in the perception of respondents, largely synonymous with repute indices.[1]

The most salient feature of this repute system is that its indices are subjective rather than technical. That is, they are subjective to a greater degree than is the case in most professions founded upon a "scientific" discipline. In the natural and biological sciences, academic professionalism evolved more or less concurrently with, and was substantially derived from, the accumulation of scientific knowledge, whose functional utility in America's material and technological progress provided a solid base for professional repute. The knowledge itself was by nature scientific, technical, and immediately applicable in a manner far surpassing that of the knowledge produced by political science at any point in its history.

The profession's repute system has a comparatively shaky foundation. Political science has chosen to call itself a "science" and, most often, a "profession" (though many prefer the designation "discipline"). "Profession" and "science" are two of the most prestigious occupational labels available and should command great deference and resources.[2] Yet, in contrast to most scientific professions, science is more a goal than a realization.

The advent of professional consciousness at this embryonic stage of scientific evolution has meant that the repute system is, to an important degree, different from those of many scientific professions. It must rely more heavily upon subjective judgments of professional peers that are less firmly grounded in scientific knowledge. Rarely, if ever, can political science look toward laws, theorems, or even accepted operational constructs to help evaluate scholarly worth. But professional and organizational dynamics demand a repute system,[3] so other sources, different from those available to established science, must be found. Scientism and repute may not be inherently synonymous, but given the public affect for professional science in America, the path of least resistance and source of greatest reward encourage a professional organization toward a "scientific' posture whenever possible.[4] The mantle of science cannot be claimed by moral philosophers who are explicit about what they are doing. The prestige of a scientific profession thus accrues to those who seek, achieve, approximate, or imitate science. It is these scholars who provide the profession with its most prestigious definition or role in terms of public perception.

The lure of the prestige of science coupled with its impressive absence in comparison to hard science means that the profession is forced to rely heavily on peer group perceptions to determine which scholars, works, and methodologies will legitimately claim "scientific" status. This ties repute to influences transcending accumulated scientific knowledge to a degree surpassing many scientific professions.

One need not—and certainly cannot—attribute a technical purity and absolute "objectivity" to professional repute in the hard sciences in order to contrast the state of political science.[5] The difference is one of degree. This analysis does not offer hard science as necessarily worthy of emulation, but simply reiterates what has been a rather constant theme in the profession's literature: that there is indeed a difference of scientific capacity between political science and, for example, physics.

An atomic physicist cannot, by himself, do much to convince the public or even his clients that he stands head and shoulders above his professional peers; his occupational specialty is too complex and technical. Nor can he convince his peers without the prerequisite use of established science existing as valid knowledge, theorems, and theories. He is not *as* free to engage in wildcat speculations in professional repute by playing to advantage the interactions of publishers, journal editors, clients, and institutions on the one hand and peer group adulation on the other. For him, the repute market is less entrepreneurial. His pursuit of repute is encumbered by the highly refined nature of his field's knowledge and of its epistemological standards and procedures.

In political science, epistemological criteria for scholarship are, in comparison to established science, either rudimentary or nonexistent. Because of this, value preference, ease of communication, and previously accrued repute play a dominant role in definitions and perceptions of what constitutes political "science."

This nebulous, subjective foundation provides no effective checks against the false orthodoxies potential in the monolithic and one-dimensional tendencies of all repute systems.[6] Authentic scientific knowledge cannot by itself prevent orthodoxy, but it can ameliorate some of the deceptions of consensual myths by confronting them with alternatives that are more contingent upon empirical reality.

Vocational Knowledge and Reliable Knowledge

The concept of "vocational knowledge" describes important aspects of the state of political science as a science.[7] It contrasts the "knowledge" which it currently produces and uses with the more rigorous, scientifically advanced, and demonstrably valid "knowledge" of the kind characterizing the natural and biological sciences. Vocational knowledge is rooted in the profession's efforts to systematically study politics, its lack of an authentically scientific store of knowledge, and the nature of its repute system. It is a conception of those epistemological limitations which the profession has yet to transcend. Reliable knowledge, in contrast, possesses certain epistemic characteristics manifested by the kind of knowledge associated with the more advanced sciences. It is termed "reliable" because its conclusions are more trustworthy in terms of rigor and validity.

Despite its epistemic limitations, vocational knowledge performs important functions. Comprising models, analogies, and taxonomic systems, it helps practitioners to make sense of political phenomena and to probe them, though it does not (and logically cannot) provide causal explanations and testable theories of the kind typical of established science. It facilitates the analysis of phenomena and conceptualization and speculation about their causes and patterned relationships, and serves as a medium of discourse within the intellectual community. Though vocational knowledge is quasi-theoretical in Meehan's sense, lacks falsification potentiality, and does not constitute scientific explanation, it can provide a heuristic base for scientific progress.[8]

Most of what the profession designates as "knowledge" and most of its scholarship are of the vocational rather than reliable type.[9] This analysis will not offer substantive examples of reliable knowledge for the practical reason that this would, in order to be accurate, demand extensive, detailed justification by means of textual exposition and epistemic scrutiny. Such an examination is not consistent with the overview of the profession and its knowledge attempted here.

The Professional Roots of Vocational Knowledge

The first generation of behavioral political scientists exhorted colleagues to pursue reliable knowledge through a commitment to theory and epistemically informed empirical research.[10] In retrospect it appears that the path to reliable knowledge proved more difficult to traverse than originally imagined. Though Easton's challenge to achieve scientific sophistication was enthusiastically pursued, it is now evident that the intensity and focus of the commitment became part of the problem and not the solution.[11] In the rush toward science, the complex problems of epistemology depicted by Easton and others were usually ignored. The crucial links between data and real theory were all but obscured by a deluge of empiricism lacking the scientific consciousness and epistemic capacity to achieve—or even point toward—reliable knowledge.[12]

The primary message of *The Political System* was that through a careful and informed attention to epistemology, the profession could close the gap between itself and the hard sciences. But there was another point, well understood long before Easton's charge, which may have been seized upon to the displacement of the epistemic challenge. The lack of rigor and reliable knowledge was, in fact, an occupational status problem as well as an epistemic one. Easton says: "However much students of political life may seek to escape the taint, if they were to eavesdrop on the whisperings of their fellow social scientists, they would find that they are almost generally stigmatized as the least advanced. They could present society, they would hear, with at least a slice of bread but they offer it only a crumb." [13]

This is the challenge that was most ardently accepted by the profession. The result has been a new posture of precision and rigor that often appears to be "scientific," or is simply accepted or defined as such, though it is in no way inclusive of the epistemic capacities of reliability necessary for authentic science. It is undeniably more precise and rigorous than the traditional institutional, descriptive, and historical kinds of approaches that previously characterized political inquiry, but this is another matter.

Vocational knowledge is in part the product of a professional process and it functions within that process despite its limitations. The most salient, non-intellectual function is that of relieving status anxieties of the type referred to by Easton. Intentionally or unintentionally, vocational knowledge provides the profession with an aura of "scientific" stature.

Epistemic Over-claim

From whatever causes, political science is currently prone to careless over-claims that tend to confuse vocational and reliable knowledge. The result is a professional culture that generally lacks a proper regard for the limitations of its "knowledge." Epistemic over-claim is the device by which political science pursues the prestige accruing to an authentically scientific profession, despite the fact that science is still more a goal than a reality.

Examples of such over-claim abound at various levels of professional culture.[14] Basic distinctions such as the one between theory and quasi-theory are frequently glossed over. One finds in the literature many quasi-theoretical works or approaches labeled "theory." *Administration in Developing Areas: The Theory of the Prismatic Society, An Economic Theory of Democracy,* and *Modern Organization: A General Theory* are three such works.[15] Moreover, categories of popular approaches, models, and conceptual schemata are often tagged as "theory." In one collection of articles drawn together to survey contemporary inquiry, advertisements of "theory" are copious: "Systems Theory," "The Theory of Decision Making," "What Is Game Theory?" "The

Analytical Prospects of Communications Theory," "The Theory of Political Development." [16] In none of these articles nor in the literature that they characterize can one find the epistemic capacities of real theory. The misleading labeling of scholarly works is not an esoteric question of semantics, for it reflects a deeper confusion about the nature of epistemology and about the state of scientific progress.[17]

Kuhn's Paradigm: Over-claim by Professional Elites

Epistemic over-claim is manifested in broad assessments of intellectual progress. In consecutive presidential addresses, David Truman and Gabriel Almond referred to an emerging "paradigm" of inquiry.[18] Assessments of the relevance of Kuhn's work pervade analyses offered by professional elites.[19] One hazard in employing Kuhn as a reference point for epistemic reckoning and exhortation is that his work is exceedingly complex and elusive, permitting, as Martin Landau warns, "diverse students to employ it as they see fit." [20] One critic of Kuhn—not a political scientist—culled no fewer than twenty-one different meanings or nuances for "paradigm" from *The Structure of Scientific Revolutions;*[21] this helps spawn the bewildering variety of interpretations and claims concerning the profession's "paradigmatic" condition.[22] Another hazard is that Kuhn's interpretation of scientific development has been severely criticized by scholars in the philosophy of science, who have persuasively challenged its accuracy.[23] These controversies are often neglected by political scientists who seek to apply Kuhn's thesis.

Almond's description of "paradigm" is revealing in what it selects from Kuhn's exposition and what it conveniently neglects. He begins with the loose interpretation that the ideological perspective of the Enlightenment is analogous to a paradigm. If one accepts this premise, it is certainly true that the behavioral revolution represented a "paradigm" shift, because it was a shift in perspective toward rigorous methodology. Kuhn, however, did not intend that his paradigm be interpreted as synonymous only with world view or even dominant methodology, but with functional theory as well.[24] A paradigm is an operational system of phenomenalistic "problem solving" possessing epistemic capacities for reliable explanation and theory. "Emerging" paradigm requires emerging theory, not solely emerging consensual myth or ideology.

Wolin is correct in asserting that "despite claims to the contrary, political science has not undergone a revoluton of the type described by Kuhn in which a new and dominant theory is installed. Although an abundance of new 'theories' is available to political scientists, it should be remembered that, by Kuhn's canon, the mere existence of new theories, or even the fact that some theories have attracted a following, are not conclusive evidence of a revolution." [25]

The crucial point is utility. What renders Almond's claims of paradigm premature is not only the vagueness of Kuhn's work, but the meager epistemic capacities of the "theories" now available in political science. The lack of consensus to which Wolin refers is precipitated by the dominance of quasi-theory. That is, a real paradigm in Kuhn's sense cannot be realized through vocational knowledge alone because the latter has no capacity for theory or for what Kuhn terms "problem solving." Lacking theory, the quasi-theoretical formulations of vocational knowledge have no ability to validate either the solutions they offer or the way in which they pose the problem, and thus cannot "solve" problems in any epistemically valid sense.

It is the profession's limited epistemic progress that makes Kuhn's model difficult to apply, and not the inherent differences between social science and the physical and biological sciences (as Almond infers).[26] Available "theories" could become consensual only through preference or orthodoxy, but not through any authentic theoretical ability, powers of reliable explanation, or "problem solving" capacity.[27] If this contention is correct, and Kuhn's paradigm is theoretically functional and concrete and does not represent merely the hegemony of one abstract perspective or ideology over others, what does the claim of paradigm imply? In the absence of an operational scientific framework, such a claim is, ipso facto, a plea for professional orthodoxy that might better realize the repute attending a scientific paradigm, even though the latter is functionally absent. Wolin points out that what is central to Kuhn's paradigm is "the enforcement by the scientific community of one theory to the exclusion of its rivals." [28] Almond becomes uneasy about the implications of orthodoxy inherent in Kuhn's exposition;[29] and for good reason.

Kuhn describes the socialization of aspirant practitioners to the dominant paradigm and depicts the latter as possessing formidable powers of self-preservation and resistance to change.[30] Paradigm change is a response to a "crisis" in which phenomenological anomalies violate paradigmatic expectation so frequently and intensely that they can no longer be ignored as aberrations. The orthodoxy of perspective and methodology created by the dominant paradigm renders acceptance of paradigm change by a scientific community a slow process of atomization that may take a generation to complete.[31]

What of political science? Almond describes the emerging paradigm as characterized by a statistical approach, differentiation and specification of variables, the concept of system, and a "multilinear theory of political development." [32] These elements are currently popular, but they have not yet demonstrated the kind of functional potential necessary for an emergent paradigm. Researchers and theorists could specify and statistically probe systemic variables of multilinear political development forever, and still not transcend implicit ideology and pseudo-scientific orthodoxy.

If marked tendencies toward orthodoxy exist in an authentically scientific paradigm, imagine the resistance to anomaly, crisis, and change inherent in consensual perspectives and modes of inquiry that are not authentically scientific. A basic characteristic of vocational knowledge is that it lacks falsification potentiality and contingency. Therefore, it is more resistant to empirical anomaly and crisis because it is never forced to confront them and to deal with them. Whether it is generated by epistemic naiveté or the lure of scientific prestige, a premature perception of paradigm emergence is dangerous. It tacitly appeals for a consensus that, in the absence of science, may evolve toward a pseudo-scientific orthodoxy indefinitely resistant to constructive change and introspection, and even to the emergence of a real paradigm.

Values and Political Inquiry

The most popular way to approach the problem of values has been through the fact-value debate. This is unfortunate because that debate has often confused the reliability of knowledge with its consequences. Complaints about value biases too often focus upon the ideological implications of inquiry rather than upon the logic of inquiry. The problem with this approach is that ideological consequences inhere in reliable knowledge too. Attacking consequences without attempting to discover whether the "knowledge" attacked is reliable lumps reliable and unreliable knowledge together in a monolithic universe of analysis. The values of knowledge are dealt with, but the value of knowledge is neglected.

Focusing exclusively (or even primarily) upon the values served by inquiry often leads to an acceptance or rejection of conclusions on the basis of value preferences alone. This is imprudent because it treats reliable, scientific knowledge and pseudo-science as equals. As such, both are judged solely according to normative congeniality, exclusive of any consideration of epistemic quality and logical warrant. Since the whole purpose of authentic science is to produce knowledge that is demonstrably more valid than opinion, myth, and speculation, abandoning judgments of *how* the value consequences of knowledge come about rejects the validity of science.

While value consequences must be examined, this alone is not sufficient. *How* the "knowledge" in question relates to certain values must also be examined. Does it do so upon the strength of the demonstrable reliability of its conclusions, or does it do so because its conclusions are merely creatures of its uncontested assumptions or implicit values? In both cases, the value consequences of the conclusions may be equally pleasing or anathematic to a given commitment or perspective, but the nature of the value "bias" is quite different in each case.

Conclusions that are mere creatures of value commitments have a dual bias that demonstrably reliable conclusions do not share. In both kinds of conclusions (and in any statement so constructed that it has significance: actually asserts something) the value consequences *are* "biased." No conclusion serves all values equally well. If it did, it would be a meaningless truism or tautology. The important difference is that unlike demonstrably reliable conclusions, those that are mere creatures of value bias are victims of the biases described by the sociology of knowledge as well. They are biased not only in consequence but in origin.

Another dimension of the relationships between values and inquiry concerns politics and public policy. One common criticism of "scientific" approaches is that methodological constraints stifle the profession's capacity to deal with important political issues and problems.[33] Authentic science and reliable knowledge do not necessarily provide or propose instant solutions to salient public policy crises or political conflicts. While this renders them more narrow (by definition) than much political philosophy or polemics, it is incorrect to assert that this constitutes, ipso fact, an inability to manifest relevance to important issues and moral dilemmas.

"Science" and "moral pholosophy" represent two distinct intellectual traditions and, in certain ways, the two purposely aim to exclude one another. But this need not lead to the acceptance of a strict dualist position, especially in the knowledgeable society, where the quality and epistemic status of "knowledge" are themselves crucial moral and political concerns. "Facts" or scientific conclusions *do* seek to displace moral philosophy, yet they often impinge upon the same consideration as that philosophy. But pseudo-facts and pseudo-science seek to do the same thing. The difference is in their method of displacement, their logical warrant for displacement, and the value motivations and biases accompanying such displacement.

The Values of Vocational Knowledge: A Professional Subsidy

A political scientist observes: "Thus we find the behavioralists are in the same boat as their enemies. Neither side can offer any good reason for its basic position." [34] This may be an over-statement, but it captures the basic "value" problem within the profession. Vocational knowledge is defended as superior in objectivity to the explicit value positions characterizing political philosophy and normative discourse. The straw-man gamesman-ship of the fact-value and behavioralist-antibehavioralist debates has made this characterization appear much more valid than it is. Critics usually insist on attacking vocational knowledge because it is not value free. This is an ineffective way to pose the issue because it allows repudiation of criticism through very standard responses that beg the real questions.

First, few behavioralists (or political scientists of any per-suasion) are now naive enough to contend that their work is totally value free. Second, indictments that vocational knowledge is not value free can be met with the retort that the critics are anti-scientific: that they are seeking to saddle empirical inquiry with a rigid and untenable logical-positivism that would render empirical inquiry so esoteric as to make political science an ex-clusively philosophical discipline.

The crux of the problem in a professional-epistemological sense is not *which* values are served by vocational knowledge, or even that such knowledge is not value free. It is rather *how* its preferred values are served. This issue has been obscured, in part because critics too often allow the defense of vocational knowledge to take up the position "Heads, I win; tails, you lose." Criticisms of the values served are rebuffed as "ideological," while criticisms of logical warrant or scientific capacity are legislated out of professional life: shunted off to scientific philosophy or metaphysics. In executing this classic obfuscation of the problem, Ithiel de Sola Pool states: "Researchers in any science are seldom very clear about the logical status of what they are doing. This is an exercise left to philosophers of science." He says further that much behavioral scholarship is avowedly preferential in its values.[35]

Nothing is more intellectually vital than determining the scientific capacity of empirical research and being cognizant of the distinction between reliable and vocational knowledge.[36] To assert that only scientific philosophers can or should make such judgments is to designate them not simply the gatekeepers of all science and knowledge, but also the only ones who can even distinguish metaphysics from science.[37] When vocational knowledge is not logically scrutinized, it frequently passes for reliable knowledge because its limitations are forgotten or never perceived in the first place. When this happens, the distinctions between science and metaphysics become blurred and epistemic over-claim is assured. Moreover, the values supported by vocational knowledge gain undeserved advantage in discourse through an aura of "science" or, at least, "objectivity" that the logical warrant of vocational knowledge cannot actually command.

Vocational knowledge appears more trustworthy than mere speculation or "philosophy," and is judged so by professional culture. The epistemological-ethical problem lies in the inherent limitations of such knowledge and in its false posture or misinterpretation as reliable knowledge. Because vocational knowledge is closer to empirical codification of value positions than to the epistemically sound conclusions of reliable knowledge, its confusion with the latter provides an unjust competitive advantage for its values.

To criticize *The Civic Culture's* revisions of the participatory democratic ideal as implicitly Burkean, or to charge that it is not value free, are ineffective challenges. Its revisions are more fruitfully characterized as vocational knowledge. When one carefully compares *The Civic Culture* with Christian Bay's *The Structure of Freedom* (from an epistemic perspective) the difference in "scientific" validity is revealed as more apparent than real.[38] While it is obvious that the value positions of the two works are vastly divergent, the major difference (beyond substance) is one of scholarly style rather than of the scientific validity of conclusions. *The Civic Culture* describes political reality in the quasi-theoretical style of vocational knowledge and qualifies its notions; *The Structure of Freedom* does not. Bay's advocacy of humanistic value priorities is, in a competitive sense, disadvantaged by the "scientific" or, at least, rigorous aura that *That Civic Culture* derives from the profession's confusions about the nature and limits of its knowledge. Such confusions impede both the pursuit of reliable knowledge and effective discourse on politics.

Beneficent Knowledge

The notion of beneficent knowledge is rooted in the epistemic state of the profession and the culture of the knowledgeable society in America.[39] Simply stated, it involves the assumption that "knowledge" will be good for cherished ideals and values: that it will not only enhance understanding of the world, but will be normatively pleasing at the same time. This constitutes an attempt to render cherished values and "knowledge" compatible through the will to believe. With the dominance of vocational knowledge, there is no problem of incompatibility similar to that which might arise from a formidable store of reliable knowledge.

Because vocational knowledge conceptualizes reality and paints pictures of it, while not at the same time being held responsible to empirical phenomena in the sense of contingency or falsification potentiality, it can always be "beneficent." It is free from any epistemic burdens that might cause it to do other than reflect the cherished values of its producers, whether unconsciously or by design. Vocational knowledge supports some values and opposes others, but in the same sense as ideology. Its various formulations may conflict, but one is free to accept or reject these on the basis of preference or prejudice alone. Vocational knowledge cannot compel a rethinking of value positions by challenging assumptions with a reliable knowledge of empirical reality.

Thus, it is "beneficent" not because it validly demonstrates that phenomenological reality is on our side—is compatible with our cherished values—but, instead, because such "knowledge" is really a case of epistemic "benign neglect." Because it tells us nothing at all that can be demonstrated to be reliable, it can always be interpreted as or crafted to be "beneficent" to certain values; it need never be disconcerting.

The assumptions of beneficence impedes the pursuit of reliable knowledge and authentic science because it warps perspectives of inquiry. Approaching phenomena with the assumption that you will find out what you desire to know only in the way you want to know it fosters the worst value biases and self-deceptions imaginable, especially given the dearth of reliable knowledge and epistemic craftsmanship within the profession. This almost mystical approach makes a psychic virtue of the epistemic limitations of vocational knowledge. It leads to "conclusions" whose ideological appeal may sustain a facade of "scientific" credibility and utility even when logical warrant and authentic scientific purpose are lacking.

Is the assumption of beneficent knowledge manifested in contemporary political science? Concerning political development, Lasswell opts not for a reliable knowledge, but for the pursuit of "knowledge" compatible with his idea of democratic values. He asserts that he agrees ". . . with those who urge that models of political development should be explicitly preferential; and that the preferred model requires an ideology of progress and commitment to a wide participation in power as a long run goal." [40] Similarly, Almond and Powell argue that "the challenge to democratic political leaders is to find a theory and strategy of political development which can put realism into the service of a more humane approach on what must be a long and uncertain voyage toward the goals of democracy and welfare." [41]

At a broader level, the argument that political science must be "relevant" to contemporary political crises is—if related to the pursuit of knowledge—assuming beneficence in a manner similar to Lasswell's and Almond and Powell's, though the substance of desired values may differ. Many of the more "radical" or critical political scientists associated with the Caucus for a New Political Science seek to reorient behavioral techniques and approaches toward the production of that "knowledge" that their value positions hold to be immediately necessary for the amelioration of current problems. Without the assumption that "knowledge" will serve as a benefactor of desired outcomes in politics and public policy, or at least that it will do them no harm, such advocacies of reorientation make no sense.

The notion of beneficent knowledge is spawned or facilitated by the epistemic limitations of vocational knowledge. But assumptions of beneficence influence (as well as reflect) the quality and direction of inquiry, by tending to seduce the pursuit of research and theory toward preferred values and away from more penetrating and open-minded approaches. By so doing, such assumptions can, at least potentially, retard the attainment of reliable knowledge by circumscribing the valuable heuristic functions of vocational knowledge. In addition, they beg (or obfuscate) some of the most crucial questions facing political science concerning epistemological and ethical responsibilities in creating and using knowledge.

VIII

Political Knowledge
and Public Policy

The public policy process of the knowledgeable society, as described by Robert E. Lane, is characterized by the professionalized application of knowledge, and by the delegation of responsibility for working out "solutions" to social problems to certain professional domains.[1]

As described previously, American society's perception of knowledge is heavily influenced by its history of progress and abundance, and by the glorification of the role of applied knowledge in that history. The resulting perspectives on knolwedge have been conducive to sustaining the assumption of beneficent knowledge.[2] This assumption has led to the pervasion of a view of the application of "knowledge" to public policy that is as mechanical as the automatic models of science described earlier. That is, the dynamics of knowledge and public policy are most often viewed as a matter of: a) finding particular knowledge that will solve a policy problem as it is posed and in an ideologically optimal manner; and b) designing a policy that will execute the wisdom of the knowledge already discovered or will implement the "solution" already perceived. Such simplistic perspectives are manifested to varying degrees at both elite and mass levels of the American knowledgeable society. Mass expectations about the eudaemonic powers of applied knowledge are often only marginally more simplistic and utopian than the conceptions of "applied knowledge" held by intellectual elites.[3]

This analysis will seek to transcend the dominant assumptions and perspectives of the knowledgeable society. The purpose is not to denigrate the positive contributions of political science, or of any other profession or body of expertise. The major contention here is not that knowledge cannot or has not functioned positively in public policy. However, unlike Lane's conception and unlike dominant cultural perspectives, this analysis recognizes

111

that there is much more to consider than simply how much "knowledge" is or is not "applied" in various policy contexts.[4]

Earlier discussions have set forth the differing capacities of various kinds of "knowledge," and the failure of political science to discern effectively these distinctions. In dealing with political knowledge and public policy, this chapter cannot now ignore the saliency of these conditions. Their unanticipated consequences for the polity of the knowledgeable society in America will be a primary concern. Because of this concern, this analysis will abjure: critical exhortations about what kinds of knowledge *must* be produced and applied, and the sanguine cataloguing of what has been produced and applied (both of which characterize much of the public policy literature in social science).[5] The basic assumption here is that the epistemic quality and capacity of "knowledge" is a crucial determinant of what it can and should do in the policy process.

Because the point of depature is the *kind* of "knowledge" brought to public policy (its epistemic capacity) rather than the substantive application of knowledge, the discussion will not deal separately with distinct arenas of policy or with various bureaucratic levels and contexts. Admittedly, the arenas of education policy and defense policy are quite divergent in terms of their political parameters, styles, interest groups, decision making processes and criteria, and influences upon the polity. It is recognized that the role of a political scientist as policy consultant is vastly different in nature and consequences in the White House basement than in the city manager's office. Yet, the perspective employed here transcends substantive or organizational context. While admitting that these have a profound influence, the major focus will be how political "knowledge" and perceptions of it interact, and influence the public policy process.

Before discussing political science itself, some important features of the relationships of social science to public policy will be set forth. The situation in political science shares much with that of social science in general. The latter's experience in public policy can be broadly characterized as one of frustration, produced by the gap between what social scientists would like to do or feel that they should do and what they have been able to do. "It is no wonder," Don K. Price observes, "that many a social scientist, looking at the spectacular accomplishments of the material scientist, begins to dream of a society in which scientific method will replace the accidents of politics or the arbitrary decisions of administrators in determining the policies of society." [6] In reality, social science is very far from actualizing such a grandiose service role, and it has devoted much effort to explaining this "failure."

It is often argued that there is a regrettable but fixed barrier between policy makers and social scientists, forged by the specialization, jargon, and ivory-tower penchants of the latter. Many treatments have sought to break down this perceived barrier through a variety of mechanisms. Sometimes, it is simply asserted that the barrier either does not exist or is not as formidable as imagined.[7] This argument usually contends that the barrier will disappear or become more permeable when one side or the other— policy makers or social scientists—comes to its senses; this will occur when policy makers become cognizant of the utility of social science as it exists, or when social scientists become sufficiently cognizant of the needs and milieu of the policy makers that they produce more useful knowledge. "Solutions" are commonly conceptualized as involving the sensitivity training of one side to appreciate the role of the other. Exhortations for reciprocity and understanding of each other usually have little or no concern for the reliability of the "product" exchanged: for the epistemic quality of knowledge. At times social science seems to fret over its public policy role in much the same manner as a soap manufacturer faced with a market crisis: the goal is to increase sales and the method is hard-sell advertising and public relations.[8] Too often, only the most tangential consideration is given to improving the product itself, beyond improving its salability.

Analysis is usually focused upon the communications and organizational links between social science and federal policy, both generally and in specific policy contexts.[9] The prescriptions and goals are typically geared toward building new bridges and/or repairing old ones. The report of the National Science Foundation Commission on the Social Sciences reflects dominant concerns about the policy role of social science.[10] It views the major impediments to a broader role as: 1) lack of clients; 2) the distinct roles of social scientist and policy maker; 3) implications that threaten the status quo; 4) financial limitations; and 5) the political process. Furthermore, the report blames social scientists themselves for their failure to work toward applied knowledge: for emphasizing the ivory-tower or pure-knowledge aspects of scholarly endeavor. Nowhere in the report does one find any meaningful cognizance of policy implications stemming from the existence of different kinds of knowledge possessing different capacities of reliability; nor is there any recognition that perceiving and dealing with such differences are themselves an important intellectual activity extremely relevant to the policy process.[11]

Frustration and disappointment generated by a meager policy involvement have led a variety of attempts to recast the service role. New careers and roles for social scientists in which they do not simply advise or seek answers but "analyze" are often advocated. Through more specified and more technical roles, such as that of "policy analyst," the hope is to become more useful to policy makers.[12] Through Planned Programming Budgeting Systems (PPBS), devices similar to it, and advances in the technology of information, these disciplines have shifted the focus of their self-perceived policy role in the direction of illuminating problems and defining alternatives, rather than providing nebulous counsel or "answers." The idea seems to be to cast the social scientist as merely another technical specialist, much like those employed by policy makers on a grand scale, whose province just happens to be policy decisions. As critics of PPBS are fond of pointing out, the lingering problem is that policy "analysis" does not necessarily render policy decisions more competent or rational, and certainly not apolitical.

The "policy analyst" role relies upon applicable knowledge with which to work. The intense commitment to "applied knowledge," which seems to be pervading contemporary American science even more than in the past, facilitates this new role. The National Science Foundation, long a patron of basic or "pure" research and more recently a significant benefactor of social science, reordered its funding priorities, hoping to "produce something useful relatively fast." [13] Many recent books written or edited by social scientists themselves to describe what they believe their disciplines can and should do in public policy manifest a heavy emphasis upon technical skills. The role depicted in these works is usually close to that of a "policy analyst." [14]

Despite all the impediments and frustrations, social scientists *are* called upon to contribute their expertise to policy formation at various levels of government. Many formal and informal links between these disciplines and policy makers exist, though their scope and consequence vary among policy contexts.[15] Political scientists are no exception. In the area of foreign policy, they are called to testify before congressional committees in greater numbers than their fellow social scientists, owing to the special relevance of their expertise.

TESTIFYING SOCIAL SCIENTISTS, CATEGORIZED BY FIELD*
January, 1959 - June, 1966[16]

FIELD	COMMITTEE		
	Foreign Relations	Foreign Affairs	Total
Total	33	35	68
Political Science	11	14	25
Economics	5	4	9
International Relations and Area Studies	11	14	25
Sociology	2	0	2
Psychology	2	3	5
Anthropology	2	0	2

*By number of appearances rather than number of persons. A total of fifty-eight social scientists have appeared at least once before one or both of the committees. Twenty-nine have appeared at least once before the Foreign Relations Committee and thirty-five at least once before the Foreign Affairs Committee.

Political Science and Public Policy

Though much attention has been given to political science's public policy role, overviews dealing with the influence of professional processes and the nature of knowledge itself are rare.[17]

Such neglect is probably fostered by the traditional view of the profession's role that long preceded the behavioralist-anti-behavioralist debate. This view is concerned with bringing available wisdom to men in power and is very conscious of the frustrations of doing so. In the decades prior to the current clash over policy "relevance," there was more attention given to how to communicate knowledge to policy makers than to how to dissect the processes and products of inquiry in search of value bias.[18] It was tacitly assumed by most scholars that the profession's knowledge would be useful, if not beneficent.

Partly because of that assumption, the traditional view has emphasized, and lamented, the incongruities between academic political knowledge and practical politics, and has tended to generate a myopic perception of the links between the two in the knowledgeable society.[19] This analysis posits that such incongruities are more useful in depicting what does happen between political science and public policy than in depicting what does not happen. Focusing on the linkage between the profession and public policy (especially at the regime level), this chapter is concerned not with organizational charts or the actual mobility of experts between academia and Washington, but, rather, with the intellectual genealogy of "knowledge."

This broadly defined "relevance" is predicted upon the functions and influences of "knowledge" in contemporary America. The focus is that of a scientific profession in the knowledgeable society, where knowledge is increasingly indispensable and anything that constitutes "knowledge" is potentially useful in the formation and implementation of public policy. The nature of the actual use and its value consequences are, or course, problematic.

Thus, it is not contended that the profession lacks "relevance" because its exprtise is not directly employed much by policy makers or because its "knowledge" serves the wrong values. Being concerned with the potential as well as actual policy influence of knowledge, the definition of "relevance" is, in contrast, much more inclusive. For example, the study of political socialization produces "relevant" political "knowledge" not only because of its potential links with counterinsurgency policy at home and abroad, but because its literature often includes Platonic speculation and advertisements about manipulating socialization processes for policy goals.[20]

While many political scientists would like their profession to have a greater policy role, there is already sufficient involvement to warrant a careful examination of the nature of its knowledge and expertise. Through myriad formal and informal contacts, political scientists *do* influence policy.[21] Still, the traditional frustrations loom large, as one scholar relates: "As a congressional fellow of this Association I tramped the halls of the house office building, offering my services as a political scientists . . . free mind you. A score of offices rejected me. In each office my stumbling block was the question 'yes, I know you are a political scientist but what can you do?' . . . In desperation I finally passed myself off as an educational expert (hadn't I taught school?) and won a desk." [22]

The emphasis upon incongruities—and antagonisms—between the political scientist and policy maker and upon the frustrations of access has impeded the profession's comprehension of the actual and potential policy uses of its vocational knowledge, as have broader, simplistic assumptions about the interactions of knowledge and politics.

"Knowledge," Politics, and Ideology

According to Robert E. Lane, public policy in the knowledgeable society is characterized by displacement of "politics" and "ideology," caused by the constant expansion of "knowledge": "If one thinks of a domain of 'pure politics' where decisions are determined by calculations of influence, power, or electoral advantage, and a domain of 'pure knowledge' where decisions are determined by calculations of how to implement agreed-upon values with rationality and efficiency, it appears to me that the political domain is shrinking and the knowledge domain is growing, in terms of criteria for deciding, kinds of counsel sought, evidence adduced, and the nature of the 'rationality' employed." [23]

With regard to ideology Lane asserts: "If we employ the term ideology to mean a comprehensive, passionately believed, self-activating view of society, usually organized as a social movement rather than as a latent half-conscious belief system, it makes sense to think of a domain of knowledge distinguishable from a domain of ideology, despite the extent to which they may overlap. Since knowledge and ideology serve somewhat as functional equivalents in orienting a person toward the problems he must face and the policies he must select, the growth of the domain of knowledge causes it to impinge on the domain of ideology." [24]

There is, however, an equally important relationship that is the other side of this argument, a side that Lane does not elaborate. Ideology and politics are just as likely to impinge upon the domain of "knowledge" as "knowledge" is likely to impinge upon the domains of ideology and politics. The neglect of this part of the knowledge-politics-ideology relationship stems from a view of knowledge as a monolithic commodity with a fairly uniform impact upon public policy. By not distiguishing among kinds and uses of knowledge, such a view tends to confuse "knowledge" with the process of bureaucratic administration.

When Lane describes "knowledge" as a domain distinctive from ideology and politics, it becomes similar in concept to bureaucracy in the traditional Weberian sense. [25] Both concepts are alike in that they manifest the major characteristics historically associated with social, political, and cultural modernity, including purposeful, highly developed kinds of organization, functional specialization, "rationality" of purpose, procedure, and criteria for evaluation, and complexity. In writing about inherent characteristics of the knowledgeable society, these are the features to which Lane refers.

In other words, "knowledge" is understood more in terms of its functions and social roots than in terms of its status in relation to science, logic, and reliability. Lane's concept has very little epistemic basis in that it neglects the specific ways in which knowledge is derived, beyond broad cultural foundations.

The evolution of systems analysis, particularly as reflected in uses of PPBS, is a good illustration of the deficiencies and hazards of such a broad and undifferentiated view of "knowledge." According to this view, PPBS qualifies as a special kind of "knowledge." It has been widely billed as a process for setting criteria that work to insulate policy decisions from partisan conflict by making them efficient and rational in terms of desired goals. PPBS, much like Lane's concept of knowledge, tends to steer the problem solver or decision maker away from the domain of ideology. Yet there appears to be growing disillusionment with PPBS as a rational policy making device,[26] which points to the fact that the relation of "knowledge" to politics and ideology is not as simple and obvious as it first appears. In many respects PPBS represents more of a change of venue for politics than an encroachment upon it. Most often, it is little more than a graphic diagram for codifying ideological preferences rather than a way of displacing such preferences. The dynamics of values, perceptions, and politics still inhere, though there may have been a change from open-ended debate to a consideration of structured, quantified alternatives.

Because Lane's concept of "knowledge" has such a strong flavor of the administrative about it, his contention that knowledge encroaches on politics in the knowledgeable society is virtually true by definition. By its very nature the knowledgeable society is heavily bureaucratized and employs calculations of "rationality" and "efficiency" as a matter of necessity, to keep the highly interdependent, complex society running. With regard to societal evolution and complexity, what Lane calls politics—the untempered pursuit of power—is simply not sufficient to perpetuate the functioning of a technocracy.[27]

Because there are in fact different kinds of knowledge with distinctive capacities and levels of reliability, and because their degree of subservience to political power or other preferred values varies greatly, Lane's concept is incomplete in both normative and analytic terms. It neglects the hard questions about the relationships of knowledge to public policy. This neglect no doubt accounts for the optimistic conclusions about the diminishing sphere of politics and ideology.[28] In contrast, this analysis holds that some of what passes for "knowledge" is in fact little different in policy consequence and epistemic quality from calculations of power. Harold Wilensky, writing about the role of "intelligence" as a special kind of knowledge, points out how durable and persistent ideology and slogans can be, even in policy situations where "'knowledge" and "expertise" are stressed:

"No one who examines the history of such doctrines as 'strategic bombing' and 'massive retaliation,' or the sad tale of foreign intervention in such places as Cuba or Vietnam, can be impressed with 'the end of ideology,' if by that we mean the end of illusions that systematically conceal social reality. And in all these cases, intellectuals have played their part in creating and sustaining the symbolic atmosphere within which men calculate. Many a brittle slogan has perpetuated a policy long outmoded." [29]

The orientation of the policy process in highly developed Western democracies has without question shifted away from ideology as Lane defines it toward a more contextual, pragmatic, and administrative approach. However, to label this new orientation "knowledge" is to lose sight of the essential distinctions among authentic science, myth, and ignorance. Had Lane asserted that the shift has been toward a less ideological, more administrative approach his case for the role of knowledge in the knowledgeable society would be much more compelling. To define knowledge as loosely as he does and still attribute to it many of the benefits of rationality and competence attainable only from more rigorously defined and epistemically sound definitions is to neglect some of the most important implications of the knowledgeable society.

In political science, the dominance of vocational knowledge renders these implications especially salient in the profession's public policy role.

The Symbolic Uses of Vocational Knowledge

Vocational knowledge *is* useful to the policy maker as a source of "expertise;" but because of its inherent epistemic limitations, it cannot serve as reliably knowledgeable expertise except in the symbolic sense. As previously described, it is not inclusive of epistemic defense mechanisms that might temper its symbolic potential to legitimize policy. These mechanisms decrease the politician's latitude in using and selecting "expertise" to support his position.

The ability of vocational knowledge to reflect almost any value position, ideology, or set of assumptions, while not being encumbered by any epistemic characteristics making it contingent upon political events, gives it vast flexibility in public policy. The plethora of vocational knowledge in political science gives policy makers broad opportunity to solicit a respected empirical codification of a value position or policy choice, which will then help to legitimate their decisions. Regardless of how often this happens, the potential is significant. Whether through a false posture as reliable knowledge resulting from a conscious or unconscious epistemic oversell by its producers; whether through a misinterpretation of its capacity by consumers that attributes to it the qualities of reliable knowledge; or whether simply through its designation as "knowledge" and through the uncritical confidence that that label often generates, vocational knowledge adds legitimacy to those policies that it is used to support.

The hegemony of vocational knowledge within the profession means that given a compatibility of values, the political scientist and policy maker can tell each other what they want to hear. The "expert" says it better, articulates it in a more intellectually persuasive fashion; yet he, like those he serves, can usually only intuit the causal outcomes of policy decisions, and can only speculate and hope that his counsel will result in means that foster the ends desired. Given the tendency of policy markers to select experts—from all fields—who are known to be favorably disposed to their own values, and given the absence of the sobering effects that reliable knowledge might provide, there is no reason to believe that the political scientist would be less myopic than those he serves or that his influence upon policy would necessarily be salutory.

The demand and respect for knowledge inherent in the knowledgeable society and confusions within political science about the nature and capacities of its "knowledge" combine to precipitate a dangerous situation for the expert role. As Harry Eckstein warns, the problem is that "scientism in politics, being a corruption of scientific culture precisely in regarding science as a solvent of all uncertanties and necessities for choice, encourages mainly scientific quacks—persons who will produce a 'system' for dealing with virtually any problem, if the customer is gullible and the fee is right; at least, it does so where there is no clear conception of the boundaries between what science must solve and politics must decide, of the sort that largely regulates the relations between politics and the natural sciences." [30]

Vocational knowledge is not purposeful quackery, but the confusions about its epistemic capacities can cause it to function as if it were. Such knowledge can be insidiously deceptive. It sometimes allows the policy maker to derive legitimating benefits of the kind accruing from authentic scientific expertise or reliable knowledge that are far more resistant to crass manipulations.[31]

Armed with vocational knowledge, the political scientist as policy consultant can forge elegant representations of the politician's goals that cannot knowingly tell how, or if, he will achieve them, but that canont tell him that realization is impossible. Thus, the producers and purveyors of vocational knowledge who possess high professional repute are always potentially useful as intellectual rhetoricians in residence. Their public policy role and their potential complicity in chicanery and policy disaster are in part shaped by the tools of their trade: by vocational knowledge.

Until knowledge becomes reliable, an independent—rather than merely legitimating—influence upon policy is, in general, all but precluded. In the event that policy makers call upon vocational knowledge in an unusually open-minded way, not merely to legitimate or to provide psychic comfort for their preconceptions, but to inform them independently of their preconceptions, the "independent" influence still does not constitute an enhancement of policy competence of the kind that can be derived from reliable knowledge. Being independent of political reality as well, vocational knowledge is still prone to legitimating policies that may prove disastrous, even if it is taken seriously or at face value by policy makers. It cannot reduce the possibility of disaster by enhancing the competence of decisions through rigorously derived conclusions. Because of its epistemic limitations and the failure to recognize them, the major potential of vocational knowledge in public policy lies in symbolizing reliably knowledgeable expertise.

Beyond the idealized view of "knowledge" held by the knowlelgeable society exists an idealized concept of "expertise." Policy makers demand and consume expertise with voracity.[32] Ideally, they do so in order to render more informed decisions. But in the knowledgeable society, expertise has a dual function. It *can* enhance the competence of policy. Yet, in the absence of scientifically informed or reliably knowledgeable expertise, there is *still* legitimacy to be garnered from consultation with "experts." Rainwater and Yancey offer an example:

"Thus the government seemed to have backed away from its earlier practice of using social science consultations in developing a meaningful and effective strategy against the northern slums. In a very real sense, the social scientists had already served their purpose insofar as they had legitimated the government's stance in that area. . . . If the heated debates at the fall planning conference were any indication, their presence at the spring conference would only threaten the peace of the meeting. Social Science had legitimized the 'Council's Report and Recommendations to the Conference' and a social science attack on the report would be quite embarrassing." [33]

The public affect for "knowledge" and enlightenment can usually be catalyzed through the use of expertise, or through the imitation of reliably knowledgeable expertise.[34]

Given the technical complexity of most knowledge, and of the policy problems to which it relates, public judgments concerning the quality or presence of expertise naturally gravitate toward repute, and tend to become synonymous with it; as does the selection of experts by policy makers. This presents a kind of paradox in professional competence that is especially relevant to the policy role of an academic profession dominated by vocational knowledge. Though a basic characteristic of professionalism is that qualitative judgment is rendered primarily by the professional peer group, as opposed to the general public or clients, the situation is, to a significant degree, reversed in the consultant or expert role. As Wilbert E. Moore points out: "The reputation, the professional success or failure of the independent practitioner, rests precisely with potential clients, who are precisely those not technically competent to judge." [35]

When the policy focus is an area in which little or no reliable knowledge exists, repute becomes, to an even greater degree, both the basis of "expertise" and the commodity exchanged in the service relationship. The more professionally prestigious the expert is, the more legitimacy he brings to policy decisions. In turn, the expert's repute is further enhanced within his profession by virtue of his consultative role, and his profession itself has the legitimacy of its service role bolstered. Though these interactions of demanding, using, and distributing repute are generic to the "expert" role, the dominance of vocational knowledge gives them new meaning and intensity.

These interactions allow the political scientist, his clients, and his profession to derive repute benefits independently of the epistemic quality or capacity of the "knowledge" brought to public policy. The same sources that generate repute within the profession's other-directed repute system may in turn employ it for their own benefit. This symbiotic relationship, which is currently unchecked by reliable knowledge, is actually aided by epistemic oversell and by confusions of reliable and vocational knowledge. Though dangerous to competent policy, confusion and oversell can still increase the supply of repute to be used and distributed. Only when policy disasters occur and become unbearable or highly visible is the lack of reliability necessarily a curse to the policy maker. Until then, it is possible for vocational expertise to effectively perform its tasks of symbolic legitimation.

Edleman's thesis that much of politics evidences symbolic functions of psychic reassurance, legitimacy, and quiescence apart from its manifest functions, and that symbolism may be not only a latent function of but a substitute for political and administrative action, is applicable in an analogous way to an expertise role dominated by vocational knowledge.[36] Such knowledge can help to legitimate policy in the public perception and can bring repute to professions and scholars though its advertised or assumed function—to bring reliable knowledge to policy—is absent. It serves as a symbol of scientific rationality even where there is none. In times of intense conflict within the political system, symbolic reassurance through "expertise" is invaluable to policy makers, beyond the epistemic quality of the "expertise" itself.

While many scholars are aware of the political roots and nature of knowledge, the mass public tends to perceive knowledge as apolitical, as anti-ideological. Vocational knowledge, with its scientific trappings, can symbolize rationality and help to depoliticize decisions even though it may be captured by implicit ideology. Its facade of scientism makes it potentially valuable, in a Machiavellian way, to the prudent politcian, but potentially more dangerous in the case of those less astute who assume that it affords them a reliable knowledge of political reality upon which to base decisions. Moynihan's experience with social science expertise in the war on poverty led him to conclude that:

". . . social science is at its weakest, at its worst, when it offers theories of individual or collective behavior which raise the possibility, by controlling certain inputs, of bringing about mass behavorial change. No such knowledge now exists. Evidence is fragmented, contradictory, incomplete. Enough snake oil has been sold in this Republic to warrant the expectation that public officials will begin reading labels. This precaution, if growing, is nonetheless far from universal. In the late 1960's the circles in New York that a decade earlier had conceived community action as a cure for delinquency, came forward with the notion that a slightly different form would cure educational retardation on the part of minority group public school children. Community control might improve the school performance of slum children. It might *not*. No one knows. It might have other effects that are quite desirable, *or* undesirable. It is a perfectly reasonable proposal to try out. But at this point in time it is almost unforgiveable that it should be put forth as a "proven" remedy for anything. About the only forecast that could have been made with any confidence could have been that the effort to impose community control would lead to a high level of community conflict, which in New York

City it has been doing, and which will presumably be the case elsewhere."[37]

The kind of policy "relevance" just described is in large measure an unanticipated consequence of the dominance of vocational knowledge and the failure to recognize its limits. Since its inception, the profession has aspired to play a key role in enhancing the competence of public policy, and not merely to legitimate it and generate professional repute. In order to realize this goal, distinctions between reliable and vocational knowledge must be recognized by both political scientists and those they serve.

Pure and Applied Knowledge

The confusions spawned through epistemic oversell and misinterpretation by the producers and consumers of vocational knowledge are exacerbated by other confusions about the interaction of knowledge and public policy. One of the most formidable of these involves the roles of "pure" and "applied" knowledge. In both political science and social science as a whole, perceptions of these roles are structured by notions of "relevance" and by assumptions of beneficent knowledge.

The profession's increasingly rigorous posture, its desire for scientific knowledge, and its basic commitment to democratic values have caused an ambivalent posture toward the issue of "pure" versus "applied" knowledge. Many political scientists are uncomfortable about what they perceive to be a trade-off between "relevance" to contemporary policy problems and the pursuit of scientific knowledge. The incompatibilities of "pure" and "applied" knowledge are complicated by the specific demands placed upon "applied" knowledge by value preferences. Three major problems of this sort are described by political scientist Duncan McRae:

- To provide intelligent advice on practical problems, the social science disciplines need to include systematic valuative discourse in a way that natural science does not.
- Applied social science (like applied science generally) differs from pure natural science in stressing valuative dependent variables that may not be closely related to the conceptual schemes

of pure science, and independent variables related to alternative choices open to the actor.

• Different roles and channels of influence are appropriate for pure and applied science; and for applied social science in democratic regimes, participation and consent on the part of those influenced are of vital significance.[38]

The above perspective on incompatibilities and value commitments manifests basic misconceptions that are related to confusions about the expertise role of vocational knowledge.

First, the assumption of beneficence is inherent, though implicitly so, in the term "applied." Whereas "pure" usually connotes esoteric scholarship that is not relevant to current problems, "applied" connotes just the opposite. This dichotomy, much like Lane's treatment of "knowledge," fails to be discriminating enough effectively to perceive and deal with the problems of knowledge. That is, just as Lane fails to ask "What kind of knowledge?", those who dichotomize "pure" and "applied" fail to ask, "Applied by whom? Applied for what purpose and with what consequences?"

Such failures are too salient to constitute more analytical oversights. More likely, they result from the assumption that in general—and allowing for a few aberrant instances—knowledge *is* beneficent. In the third problem listed above, it is significant that "applied" social science is prescribed as intimately linked to the democratic process and its values. It makes little sense, in normative terms, to bemoan the dearth of "applied" knowledge unless the assumpton is held that "application" will generally serve or be beneficent to preferred values. In the first problem it is asserted that social science must be purposely related to "valuative discourse." In the third, we find that the preferred values are those of Western democracy. Simply specifying what applied knowledge should do cannot eliminate the fact that:

• Some applied knowledge may not be beneficial to democratic values because its wisdom may militate against their extension or viability.[39]

• Some applications of "knowledge" can be anti-democratc, involving the symbolic manipulation of the ethos of knowledge and enlightenment to legitimate and depoliticize decisions. In such instances, values of "participation" amid "consent," which were cited as preferred in the third problem listed, may be severely compromised rather than benefited.

The dichotomy of "pure" versus "applied" not only harbors the assumption of beneficent knowledge, but seeks to readmit a science of values through the back door. The real distinction between "pure science" and "applied science," the argument goes, is that the latter is relevant in a way that the former is not. Both, however, are presumably "scientific": of similar epistemc quality and orgin. "Applied" science is, in consequence, a round-about way of assuming that science can and will tell us what we need to know to solve our problems. Because applied science is most often assumed not only to solve problems but to do so in a manner supportive of preferred values, the notion of a science of values is readmitted.

Whereas the more traditional advocacies of a science of values assume that science can provide proper values through its knowledgeable conclusions,[40] the "applied science" notion usually assumes that the knowledgeable conclusions will provide scientific direction and support for those values already preferred. Here we have come full circle to readmitting the worst value biases depicted by the sociology of knowledge; "science" again becomes subservient to values. The endless debate over the goals of science occurring within the framework of the pure-applied dichotomy is an amalgam of confusions and assumptions which exacerbates misperceptions of vocational knowledge.

Fundamental misconceptions about the nature of science dominate considerations of "pure" versus "applied" knowledge. The most salient is the idea that goals of inquiry have little or no effect upon the attainment of science, As previously described, because "pure" and "applied" presumably differ not in scientific quality but in utility, the assumption inheres that the world is so structured that there are scientific answers to be found for the questions we feel we must ask, and, furthermore, that the answers will fit the questions as we pose them. This assumption is misleading whether the goal of inquiry is knowledge for its own sake or knowledge for an immediate purpose. It is precisely because we do not know the answers, do not know what empirical reality holds for us, that the dichotomization of "pure" and "applied" knowledge is deceptive.

It is certainly true that some inquiries that lack an immediate goal for knowledge may never be useful to public policy. It is also true that the policy problems of the day usually pose empirical questions in a manner that cannot be effectively pursued by authentic science. Policy problems often involve, at base, such questions as "How can we maximize our preferred values, given conflicting priorities?" Using this as a perspective for the pursuit of scientific knowledge is likely to prove as foolish as trying to generalize artificially induced anxiety syndromes in Rhesus monkeys to the behavior of a polity. The point is that to produce scientific knowledge, one must perform similar epistemic tasks in similar ways and achieve similar results (in epistemic terms), regardless of whether the knowledge sought is "applicable." Since a primary task of epistemic craftsmanship is to proceed from a scientifically conscious posing of the problem, the emphasis upon "applied" knowledge can, if it results in the subservience of inquiry to values, retard the production of reliable knowledge.

Some "pure" knowledge may turn out to enhance the competence of policy even though it does not provide the answers posed by policy questions. "Applied" knowledge may enhance the competence of public policy, but this depends more upon how it is applied and what its epistemic capacity is than upon the fact that it was originally pursued because it was deemed useful. The perspective of "pure" versus "applied" is a dangerous oversimplification which fails to appreciate the complex problems inherent in the public policy role of an academic profession dominated by vocational knowledge. This is not to say that political science cannot or should not pursue relevant knowledge; but, rather, that it must be recognized that the validity of knowledge is not assured by its "relevance."

Relevance and Reliability

Because the profession has a focus that is expressly political, many political scientists feel it has (or should have) a special relevance to public policy.[41] "Relevance" is a perspective applicable only to the focus of research and not to the epistemic quality of inquiry. "Relevant" knowledge may or may not be reliable, but this is not determined by its "relevance." "Relevance"—in the sense of a focus upon current political and social problems and their solution—neither precludes nor assures reliability.

One can argue that political science ought to be more relevant, though the notion that this is necessarily conducive to justice or radical change is naive. Theodore Lowi contends that relevance is shaped by the inherent nature of problem solving in a technocratic society, which he views as basically "conservative." He cautions those who exhort that increased relevance will bolster values of justice and egalitarianism: "Thus a political science dedicated to better solutions to society's problems cannot in the long run be radical or science, because it will be too closely tied to the very regimes whose roots it must constantly question." [42]

Regardless of the values served by relevance, one cannot logically argue that reliable knowledge, established theories, or valid explanations *ought* to be more "relevant," because such an assertion is utopian and anti-scientific. That is, in arguing that the reliable products of inquiry are deficient because they are not "relevant," one is merely second-guessing or rejecting the demonstrated configuration of empirical reality. One may second-guess or criticize the focus or conclusions of vocational knowledge without concurrently rejecting demonstrated configurations of empirical reality. Vocational knowledge says nothing about that reality that it can reliably demonstrate. Insisting upon a change of focus for vocational knowledge to one more ideologically pleasing, is not necessarily anti-scientific or utopian.

This is not the case with reliable knowledge. It cannot (in both the logical and normative senses) be rejected merely because it does not produce desired solutions or conclusions. If "relevance" is used as a moral argument to reject knowledge merely because the consequences of that knowledge are disconcerting, then it is simply a fancy way of codifying ideological displeasure. As such, it has no logical relationship to the analytical evaluation of knowledge. It is illogical to argue that reliable knowledge must deal with certain variables in certain ways and produce certain results, because reliable knowledge cannot be shaped to our wishes. Arguing that it *must* do certain things is, at base, not a critique of the narrowness of scientific approaches, but, rather, an implicit plea for pseudo-science or a statement of faith in the beneficence of knowledge.

The Political Scientist, the Policy Maker, and Science

The pursuit of a scientific knowledge of political life cannot be conducted in isolation from the political process. Because the profession is still in the formative stages of its search for reliable knowledge, contact with real politics is useful in posing the questions which that knowledge will seek to answer. This contact also serves to expand our cognizance of the range and scope of political phenomena, whether "pure" or "applied" knowledge is sought. However, such contact is not an absolute blessing for the pursuit of science and reliable knowledge at either the collective or individual level.

Individual political scientists and the profession as a whole may engage in certain kinds of political interaction that miltate against science rather than inform its pursuit. Chapters V and VI argued that authentic science could not be achieved merely by an objective orientation. This is not to say that individual orientations are not important or do not shape inquiry. It cannot be precisely determined *which* modes of political contact benefit science and which impede it without the help of an extensive clinical survey. No fixed criteria for such distinctions exist, for this is a complex problem of psychological dynamics. Yet, some confining premises of beneficial contact with real politics can be hypothesized, based upon the exigencies of authentic science.

The "detachment" of a researcher is not sufficient for the attainment of science, but some degree of it is necessary. Stated very simply, extreme—or perhaps even ponderous—involvement in politics is not conducive to epistemic craftsmanship, regardless of the ideology or values served. The political scientists who is a presidential policy advisor much or most of the time is simply too enmeshed in the problems and priorities of real politics to consider those of scientific inquiry. Even if he attempts to be "objective" or "scientific" in retrospect (after his involvement is terminated), it is likely that the psychological effects of commitment and participation will heavily bias his analysis.

The sociology of knowledge tells us that the intellectual insights produced in situations of intense participation serve many masters: organizational structure, ideology, self-interest. The pursuit of reliable knowledge may be served. This analysis cannot logically rule this out because it has previously asserted that it is not the source of insight that determines scientific quality, but, rather, the epistemic procedures that follow it. Still, given a situation of extensive and demanding involvement, the priorities of the political scientists' perception and thought are such that insights of the kind most needed by authentic science are an unlikely by-product.

Escape from value bias and myth is difficult, even when the intellectual is not subject to the powerful influences over thought generated by strong political commitment. Thus, to the extent that a political scientist shoulders a heavy policy burden or becomes a full-time intellectual apologist or political activist, he is unlikely to be, at the same time, effectively pursuing reliable knowledge. This is not posited to be an intellectual contamination that necessarily lingers; it pertains to the scholar's thinking during such involvement and to his later use of this experience.

Scientific insight is an improbably result of sustained personal activity in political movements or protests. While the self-interest stakes, values, and dynamics of this kind of involvement differ from those of a governmental service role, the effects upon the process of inquiry are similar. Whether the perspective on phenomena that the political scientist adopts is derived from a radical opposition to existing institutions or from the problems and goals of governing elites, the posing of questions and seeking of answers are not apt to be compatible with epistemic craftsmanship and scientific consciousness.

At the collective level there is a tension between the development of reliable knowledge and an extensive commitment to societal problem solving. As stated throughout this analysis, such tension results from the clash of goals and perspectives of these two orientations to the search for knowledge. As Lowi put it: "To help the policy maker solve problems is to make the conduct of his responsibilities a good deal more comfortable. And the problem and the solution are made more legitimate by virtue of the academic help rendered him. But *most importantly, it means that the intellectual agenda of the discipline is set by the needs of the clientele, not by the inner logic of political science.*" [43]

Toward A
Professional Ethic

Ethics is an extremely perplexing area within academic professions. Intellectual freedom is in constant tension with norms regulating the production and use of knowledge and the activities of professionals. Ethical complexity is compounded by the many kinds of professional roles in an academic discipline. A broad and consistent ethical approach is compelled to deal with several interrelated areas: professional role, conduct, and certification; professional culture and processes; relationships with clients and publics; and standards for and definitions of "knowledge" and "science," and methodological norms and goals for their pursuit.

The linkages among these areas, and their diversity, render the development of broad and consensual ethical constraints exceedingly difficult, especially in political science, which manifests conflicting values in all of them. This ethical morass has fostered three pervasive but inadequate responses.

One response is to proclaim that academic professions constitute an exception to the problems and dynamics of conventional "professional ethics" because they deal with concerns that are strictly intellectual.[1] This distinction is often employed as an argument for ethical laissez-faire, for abjuring any collective codes, policies, or even guidelines. While the processes of a knowledge-based profession are to some extent unique, this does not obviate the ethical significance of the network of client and public relationships that these professions have developed in recent decades.[2]

The second response avoids the larger, more involved issues by compartmentalizing ethical concerns in terms of origin, responsibility, or substance. This is manifested by the American Political Science Association's committee on professional ethics, through its advisory opinions dealing with specifically defined problems (manuscript submissions, hiring, the propriety of acknowledgments).

The third response is to structure an overarching ethical framework by imposing an ideological or extra-professional gestalt upon the professional sphere. "Radical," redistributive ideology has been put forth by some political scientists as ethically relevant to the profession's external relationships, epistemological debates, and internal dynamics.[3]

One of the most demanding tasks is to craft a viable ethic that deals with the multi-faceted nature of professional life, that is explicitly professional in focus and genesis, and that does not arbitrarily restrict freedom and creativity. The assumption here is that neither the compartmentalization of ethical concerns nor the transplantation of extra-professional value frameworks can be as effective in understanding and ameliorating ethical problems as an explicitly professional ethic that is broadly cognizant of epistemic, service, and occupational conditions. Such conditions are, to an important degree, unique to each academic profession at a given point in time.

Ethical Problems in Academic Professions: Vignettes

Despite the bewildering nature of the ethical morass, academic professions *do* attempt to deal with ethical problems. Though the latter are inexorably linked, professions tend to perceive and to deal with ethical spheres separately and selectively.[4] This approach is not peculiar to epistemologically underdeveloped disciplines like political science, but is apparent in the hard sciences as well.

One ethical focus that has a special prominence in political science is that of value consequences: what values are sustained, opposed, or neglected by the pursuit of knowledge, service relationships, and professional processes?[5] The preeminance of these kinds of concerns is nowhere more evident than in the furor precipitated by the bizarre and abortive "Project Camelot." Ethical reactions were primarily aimed at the values served: the manipulation of political systems for purposes of counterinsurgency was a goal abrasive to the ideological sensitivities of social scientists. Responses rarely originated in epistemologcal perspective: criticism of the absurdly grandiose and pseudoscientific nature of social science involvement, given the limited and unreliable state of its knowledge about manipulating macro-political outcomes.[6] Most reactions were so overtly ideological that it appears that a "Project Robin Hood," aimed at egalitarian, redistributive manipulations of political systems, would have created few ethical shock waves.

The centrality of value consequences is not limited to social science. From the classic dilemma of physicists working on the Manhattan Project to the debate over the ethics of medical testing, judgments are typically cast in terms of value consequences and priorities. In defending the ascendance of scientific-professional values in experimentation on humans, a medical researcher contends: "It is my feeling that western civilization accepts medicine as an experimental discipline and that, in expecting it to continue to grow, to be a progressive science, as against the attitudes of the medicine man whose incantations and medicaments were not expected to nor designed for change, an acceptance of the trail of the new and the search for the better is implicit. I also think that when society confers the degree of physician on a man it instructs him to experiment on his fellow. I then choose to believe this covers both categories of consent, the straightforward as well as the experiment which does not benefit the subject." [7]

Another focus for ethics is that of the activities of professionals (the roles they play inside and outside the profession, and the conflicts these produce). In political science, such conflicts are typically approached from the perspective of incompatible values, but the accompanying ethical problems are often posed in terms of the activity itself rather than the inherent value consequences. Two salient problems germane to this focus have to do with political activity and governmental service.

Under what conditions does "political activity" violate norms of professional conduct? Conversely, when do professional norms unjustly circumscribe individual political freedom? These are difficult judgments in times of protest and violence. Most statements from academic professions (particularly those from the American Political Science Association) have relied heavily on the

American Association of University Professors guidelines, and have tended to define the problem as one of opposing roles: citizen and activist versus professional, analytical scholar.[8] No report issued by the American Political Science Association or its committees has come to grips with the difficult task of adequately defining role boundaries or offering viable criteria for settling role conflicts.

Very often the profession's discourses on the political activities of its members confuse the posing of the problem with its resolution. For example, it is often asserted that the key distinction between legitimate political activity and violation of professional ethics is whether the political scientist acts as an individual citizen, or, in contrast, acts in such a way as to fuse his activist and professional roles. It is argued that in the latter case he misappropriates professional prestige, because he is perceived by the public to "know" more about issues than the ordinary citizen knows. This principle may be useful as an ideal construct, but how can it be applied on any rational basis not dominated by the ideological biases that it presumably aims to supplant? Does it require that professional status be explicitly disclaimed within the context of any "political" activities? If so, how does this relate to the telegram in which all past presidents of the Association since 1964, the then president, and the president-elect state:

"Acting in our individual capacities as political scientists who are devoting their lives to the study of politics we are impelled by the present crises to offer our considered professional advice for the quickest, most effective way of saving lives in Indochina and reducing strife at home. One course alone remains: an immediate and clear commitment to a rapid and orderly withdrawal of all American armed forces from Indochina to be substantially underway by December, 1970, and to be completed by July, 1971."[9]

This statement, published in the *American Political Science Review,* raises some knotty issues concerning role differentiation. Is the disclaimer of individual capacity viable when the presidents of an assocation of learned persons, using as their medium of communication its most prestigious journal, openly offer "considered professional advice" linked to a devotion of their lives to the study of politics?

The attempt to have the American Political Science Association take some stand on the "ethics of political scientists in high office" (a resolution declared unconstitutional by the presiding officer of the 1973 annual business meeting, and judged so by the majority of those present and voting) and the proposed investigation of "aspects of Dr. Henry A. Kissinger's public conduct" (a resolution withdrawn by its sponsor at the same meeting) are examples of the focus on governmental service.[10]

The third sphere of ethical concern involves methodological-epistemological criteria. Again, this focus is intimately linked to value consequences and professional activities, but it reflects a different emphasis in the posing of the problem: perceived abuses or distortions of those methodologies or epistemic canons that are dominant within an academic profession. In social science the confused, often rudimentary, status of methodology and epistemology in comparison to hard science makes ethical judgments all the more complex, and precipitates charges that epistemological condemnations are ideologically motivated.

A classic case of this type derives from a study entitled "A Profile of the Aging: USA" written by two sociologists in 1960.[11] It clearly refuted a huge body of social science research conducted during the 1950's that had become the intellectual legitimation for Medicare advocacies. Because the study appeared during the height of the Medicare debate, was funded by the Foundation For Voluntary Welfare, and was swiftly appropriated by the American Medical Association to help in its campaign against Medicare, a flurry of criticism ensued, ranging from methodological challenges to charges of intellectual prostitution.

The attack by social scientists was primarily aimed at methodology. Critics proposed the creation of a review panel of prominent sociologists to search out methodological errors or subterfuges. The American Sociological Association declined, fearing that such a quasi-investigatory foray into scholarly research would set a precedent hostile to intellectual freedom. While the study manifested some obvious biases in sampling and research design that contributed to its sanguinary conclusions, the epistemological consciousness and rigor brought to its evaluation were neglected with regard to the bulk of research that supported the opposite side of the Medicare debate. Moreover, the visceral nature of reactions left little doubt that the methodological attacks were ideologically inspired. The instance illustrates that the application of epistemic canons to ethical problems can raise more ethical and professional issues than it solves.

This situation is not peculiar to social science. Social scientists, many of whom stand in awe of the exact nature of hard science, tend to forget that it is often at the knowledge frontiers of hard science that ethical problems arise. It is there that the precision and rigor that characterize the normal work of a scientific community may be severely limited—or lacking altogether. "Different people," as Jerome Weisner explained to President Kennedy, "make different assumptions about all these elements. That is what is involved in the argument about anti-ballistic-missile systems. One man's assumptions give one set of conclusions; another man's assumptions are essentially undefinable—we are talking about things we do not and cannot know anything about, no matter how we try. And so you can take whichever set of assumptions you choose." [12]

It is not surprising that the use of methodological-epistemological criteria to settle ethical questions has proved difficult (if not impossible) even in the most advanced sciences.[13] This is illustrated by the bitter clash within the scientific establishment following the ABM debate. The Operations Research Society of America (ORSA)— a group of some eight thousand scientists engaged in defense and industrial research—was asked by proponent Albert Wohlstetter, a former top executive at the Rand Corporation, to review the use of controversial evidence.

A six-man panel, which included both proponents and opponents, concluded that the evidence was in many cases "misleading," "factually in error," and "inappropriate"; and held that three leading opponents—Jerome B. Weisner, George W. Rathjens, and Steven Weinberg—had been guilty of misusing scientific data in their critique of the Pentagon's arguments.[14] The panel further

charged that Weisner and Weinberg had ascribed "official validity" to calculations that had none. ORSA received a letter from
presidential advisor Donald Rumsfeld praising the investigation,
which politicized the controversy even more.

Weisner, Rathjens, and Weinberg countered that the panel's
findings were false, part of a well-orchestrated effort to discredit
their testimony, which they claimed had been instrumental in holding down spending for new weapons development.[15] They asserted
that the panel was itself less than objective or thorough in its use of
evidence, having failed to give proper attention to inaccuracies and
distortions in the Pentagon's pro-ABM position (as expounded by
John S. Foster, chief scientist for the Department of Defense),
and that the panel had been grossly selective in surveying the
classified data that had been used to discredit the stand of the
ABM opponents. Finally, Weisner alleged that at least one member of the panel, Herbert Berger, was venting personal animosities
against him through the report. Regardless of the validity of the
various charges and countercharges, it is clear that professional
watchdog functions are not depoliticized by the presence of a
highly advanced epistemology.

Epistemic Canons and Professional Ethics

Though ethical problems have varied foci, the presence,
absence, and nature of epistemic canons within a knowledge-
based profession create a set of conditions that pervades the entire
range of ethical concerns. Epistemic canons are much more than
"tools of the trade"; they play a major role in shaping both internal and external professional dynamics. For example, recruitment of aspirant professionals in political science is notoriously
haphazard,[16] in part because our epistemic framework fails to
provide a convenient pattern of prerequisite education or training. Social scientists have traditionally had difficulty in getting
policy makers to listen to their "expertise," partly because of the
apparent lack of rigor in theory and research in comparison to
hard science.[17] Though the state of epistemology is crucial to
ethical problems, its impact is far from self-evident.

Political scientists, tending to blame their epistemological malaise for nearly all professional and intellectual problems, often assume that the epistemological and ethical millennia are synonymous. That is, that a science of politics approximating hard science would, ipso facto, ameliorate or solve the most perplexing ethical issues. In part this view is sustained by simplistic assumptions about the distinction or dichotomy between "facts" and "values," by confusions of reliable and vocational knowledge, and by denial of the value consequences inherent in any theoretical standards and scientific procedures. As the ORSA investigation indicates, there is little to suggest that hard scientists are far better off in coming to grips with the ethical and political dimensions of their enterprise. Regarding the American scientific community, Joseph Haberer concludes:

"There is no significant carryover of the methodological ethic into the institutional realm. Members of the community have in the past related to each other for the most part only in accordance with the canons of the methodological ethic. But this ethic has little bearing on the political, social, and interpersonal relations within science nor do they provide any guidelines for dealing with the external social and political order. Almost no guild, no community ethic has been developed. Until very recently, scientists simply did not concern themselves with the task of developing a binding institutional ethic for no major issues seemed to arise which would call for it." [18]

Despite the confusions surrounding the work of Thomas Kuhn and other revisionists of the history of science, and despite the debates concerning its precise application to political science, the relevance of Kuhn's thesis to considerations of epistemological-ethical dynamics is profound.[19]

He describes scientific development in the hard sciences as a series of "gestalt switches" and "conversion experiences" in which competing "paradigms" vie for dominance until one is embraced by a scientific community, and then "enforced." This raises serious doubt about the coincidence of epistemological advancement and ethical neutrality. If Kuhn is right, the canonical base for professional ethics in a highly developed scientific community is more stable and effective not because of its logical transcendence of value conflicts, but because the consensus and enforcement that sustain it tend to obscure such conflicts (or render them moot in a professional sense). Epistemic canons may strictly order professional ethics, but in a manner analogous to that of a consensual ideology or religious ethic that might be transplanted upon a scientific community. One need not embrace an extreme relativist position (endorsing Mannheim's "paradox" or logically discounting the objectivity of science) in order to recognize that the assumed ethical payoffs of epistemological sophistication need careful analysis.

Within political science, there exists no professional consensus about the relationships of epistemic canons and ethics, any more than there does with regard to epistemic canons themselves. More troublesome than the absence of consensus are the inadequate, often simplistic, conceptions of the ethical relevance of such canons that dominate debates. These conceptions seem polarized between an almost mystic faith in the ameliorative powers of certain epistemic canons on the one hand, and, on the other, an intellectual apartheid between ethics and epistemology.

A classic manifestation of the latter is Heinz Eulau's position expounded in *The Behavioral Persuasion.* He claims that behavioral research is value free at least in the sense that "even if the scientist sees his work as being in the service of goals that he himself cherishes, there is nothing in his science that prevents its being used for ends with which he disapproves." [20] Eulau dispenses with a host of ethical problems by falling back on the absence of scholarly omnipotence as an ethical cart blanche, a position that neglects the crucial role of professional standards in shaping the uses and abuses of knowledge and expertise. Logically, Eulau's position condones any manner of intellectual chicanery so long as the perpetrator is not sure whom he is deceiving.

Another response is to write epistemological concerns out of professional life, as does Ithiel de Sola Pool: "Researchers in any science are seldom very clear about the logical status of what they are doing. This is an exercise left to philosophers of science." [21]

"Logical status" is not simply an esoteric concern of ethical gadflies, but the key determinant of whether researchers are producing "science" or ideological exegesis, or whether they have attained reliable knowledge. Meehan tersely states the ethical implications of contentions such as de Sola Pool's:

"The fact is that a 'live and let live' attitude toward the methodological foundations of inquiry is inexcusable; good reasons can be given for accepting some methodological premises and rejecting others—reasons that a competent critic would be forced to accept. For that reason, the breakdown of communications between methodologists and social scientists, or more precisely, the failure to establish such lines of communication, has created a situation in social science analogous to the circumstances in which a physician could continue to treat a particular disease by a method known to be unproductive, or even injurious, without drawing criticism from his peers." [22]

At the opposite extreme, there is the notion that the logical positivist model of inquiry, transplanted intact or customized, will effectively solve many ethical problems. The inadequacies of this view are twofold. First, there are the implicit warnings from the work of Kuhn and others that epistemological-ethical dynamics in the established sciences may not be as trustworthy or straightforward as is often assumed. Second, there is considerable doubt as to whether the profession has a sufficient awareness of the epistemological consequences of the particular positivist canons that it seeks to import.[23]

Recent debates within the philosophy of science between positivists and relativists and within political science over the appropriateness of positivist models of explanation, hypothesis testing, and science in general are difficult to sort out, but they clearly demonstrate that neither the epistemic nor ethical payoffs of positivism ought to be taken for granted.[24]

The Behavioral Persuasion in Ethics

Though epistemic canons and models are far from consensual, the preeminence of the behavioral approach and its claims to rigor (or science) render it a primary source of epistemic canons and ethical standards, at least potentially. Contentions by such notables as Gabriel Almond and David B. Truman that the behavioral approach constitutes an emerging Kuhnian paradigm ascribe to it (at least implicitly) a dominant role in canonical-ethical dynamics.[25] Despite the accomplishments of behavioralism, both behavioralists and non-behavioralists should be skeptical of attempts to employ it as a paradigm to be "enforced" in Kuhn's terms or as a provider of the epistemic criteria for professional ethics. Behavioralism is ill suited for such a role not simply because it is not value free or because it may harbor certain value biases, but because its epistemological status is unclear if not suspect. If the comparatively precise and consensual epistemologies of hard science fail to exorcise value conflicts and ideological biases from professional ethics, why should political science risk ethical and scientific orthodoxy by turning to behavioralism as the primary source of ethical/epistemic standards? The behavioral approach is plagued by deficiencies that vastly increase the risks of pseudoscientific retardation of intellectual progress and of arbitrary circumscription of intellectual creativity. David C. Legee's harsh assessment of its methodological-epistemological status may or may not be overstated, but it serves as a reminder that behavioralism is far from attaining its goals of scientific rigor:

"A quarter of a century after the behavioral revolution in the social sciences scholarly journal articles and books by political scientists are still replete with the most gross examples of lack of awareness—conceptualization with no attention to operations or, at the other extreme, definitional operationalism, use of single indicators, lack of attention to method effects, designs with no controls over the extraneous sources of variance, face validation by one's colleagues or students, causal modelling with no attention directed to measurement error, generalizing to an inappropriate universe, etc. ad nauseam. One is still tempted to characterize our cumulative body of knowledge as a noncumulative heap of insights and artifacts."[26]

The caveats that vocational knowledge is the most rigorous that we have or that a science of politics may never achieve the strict rigor of the hypothetico-deductive models of hard science because we deal with human phenomena may be legitimate as cautions against rigidity or as exhortations not to abandon the pursuit of "science." They should be dismissed, however, as arguments for codifying behavioralism's epistemic assumptions (an concurrently its confusions and deficiencies) as professional standards, and then granting them overriding deference in ethical judgments, or employing them in a strict sense to render such judgments. To use any set of epistemic canons as professional norms for ethics or inquiry is inherently difficult and hazardous. But the potential for bias and pseudoscientific orthodoxy inimical to understanding is increased when such canons are capable of harboring ideological biases and erroneous assumptions to an even greater degree than in hard science.

Perspectives and Caveats For A Professional Ethic

A survey of the ethical problems commonly talked about in social science would lead one to believe that ethics has little to do with knowledge itself. Prominent, though not necessarily distinct, ethical concerns include:[27] the values served by research; the relationships between researcher and sponsor; the confidentiality of data; the relationships between the researcher and his respondent or subject, and the consequences of those relationships; the impact of governmental or foundation intervention in social research; questions of academic freedom; and the blatant fabrication or improper manipulation of data or findings. It is significant that only the last focuses upon the "product" rather than upon producers, consumers, or their interaction. Is crass manipulation and fabrication the only important ethical problem involving the product itself? Professional ethics has largely neglected the *claims* of scholarship; what it claims to be and to do.

Neglect is due, in part, to the hesitancy of professional organizations to become mired in the ethical morass. Perhaps there are pragmatic reasons for such reticence. First, professions come by their resources of status and repute only after an arduous struggle for public recognition and deference. Ethical violations can tarnish professional image and are then damaging to public confidence and to the faith of clients. Therefore, it is not within occupational self-interest to engage in muckraking in a highly visible way. Second, social science is a rather nebulous enterprise. To single out any scholar or scholars as personally culpable or corrupt, while overlooking collective ethical problems, is always arbitrary in such a vaguely defined intellectual context. As the preceding vignettes illustrate, a good case can often be made that the motives for castigation derive from ideological vendettas. Dubious and selective ethical condemnation conflicts with notions of academic freedom and with the liberal ideal of the marketplace of ideas, which are often more strongly cherished than any professional norms.

Fears of professional orthodoxy and intellectual repression are often precipitated by ethical issues and rightly so. No one wants the specter of McCarthyism to reappear in professional guise. Moral witch hunts have a devastating impact upon the production of knowledge, and no academic profession can function effectively under such conditions whether the target group is defined ideologically or methodologically.

Recognizing these dangers should not lead to a tacit endorsement of the present manner in which political science faces its ethical problems. The consequence of political knowledge in the knowledgeable society are too important to be neglected merely because they are linked to difficult ethical problems which are potentially dangerous to professional solidarity. The dangers of not perceiving and dealing with such problems are equally great, and perhaps greater in terms of their consequences for scientific development and public policy.

Because the nature of knowledge and orientations toward it constitute the major internal influence upon scientific capacity and public policy roles, "knowledge" *is* the key focus for ethical criteria. This is not to say that knowledge and perceptions of it create all important ethical dilemmas, or that providing such criteria will "solve" ethical problems. Still, "knowledge" is of primary importance in determining what the profession actually does and what it can do. The central ethical problem is not individual or collective venality of political scientists, but one of confusion, generated by the nature of the profession's epistemology, the state of its knowledge, and its failure to be fully cognizant of the limits of both.

Tempering existing modes of policy "relevance" and improving the profession's ethical posture do not necessitate orthodoxy, either in values or methodology. The professional ethic toward which the following prescriptions aim is not founded upon the perspective on valid explanation offered in Chapter VI, nor upon behavioralism or logical positivism. Instead, it is based upon the recognition that differences in the epistemic roots and capacities of "knowledge" are crucial. Any ethical criteria, however tentatively or circumspectly offered, are bound to draw much criticism. The issues to be dealt with are extremely volatile and exist at the core of what are often acrimonious methodological and ideological conflicts. There are, however, certain realities of political science as an academic profession which help to define the characteristics of a viable ethic.

Because its focus is so intimately related to the political process, many political scientists view the profession as an arena of ideological struggle. An ethic cannot serve one ideology or set of values and still be a "professional" rather than a political ethic. If this means that a viable ethic will disappoint many who are intensely concerned, because it does not attempt to deal with the injustices of political life, so be it. In comparison to ideology, is must be "narrow" and even "unconcerned" about political outcomes. These labels need not be pejorative if it is recognized that the profession is in important ways distinct from the political system, even though linked to it.

Any ethical prescription is open to accusations that it is too utopian or, conversely, that it attempts too little. The basis for such charges is usually an ideological rather than professional gestalt, which makes them accurate by definition. If the indictment of "utopianism" is directed at the likelihood of "implementation" or "enforcement," it misses the point. In a professional community seeking knowledge, "enforcement"—in the legal, authoritative sense—is both impractical and undesirable. It is impractical because salient problems are too subtle and complex to lend themselves to effective "policing" of any kind. It is undesirable because the very notion of "enforcement" mechanisms is inimical to the freedom, creativity, and even eccentricity of endeavor upon which the pursuit of knowledge thrives. Charges that a professional ethic is too bland or attempts too little are sometimes deficient for similar reasons: its scope and intensity must necessarily be limited, given the absence of effective enforcement, the dangers of orthodoxy, and the heterogeneity of values, ideologies, and professional orientations among those to whom it is attempting to bring some modicum of consensus. It must be sensitive to such exigencies or leave enduring ethical problems unaffected in any meaningful way.

On the Nature of Responsible Scholarship

The notion of "responsible" scholarship furnishes an association between a professional ethic and moral implications stemming from the use and nature of political knowledge.[28] In this context, "responsible" has no substantive connotation; it simply refers to how political scientists perceive and describe their work, whatever it may be. Responsibility is not connected to any particular values, ideology, or epistemic canons. It cannot, even ideally, guarantee that the uses of political knowledge will be "democratic" or "rational." Responsibility does not demand that a political scientist demonstrate "certain" knowledge before he advances claims or exhortations.[29] Nor does it dictate that rigorous empiricism and value discourse cannot appear within the same format. It does not mean that the only proper role is that of a sober, "factual" analyst whose humility and epistemic sophistication compel him to take no stands on issues and to say nothing of political significance; nor does it preclude polemics or feckless speculation.

Responsibility does mean that neither the conduct of inquiry nor professional prestige and expertise should be employed—consciously or unconsciously, through malevolence or ignorance—in deceptive ways. Simply stated, scholarship (and the public and intellectual regard that it commands) must not be perverted in order to advance claims or support values or ideologies. "Perverted" is purely professional in connotation and applies not to the values served by deception or to the misconduct by non-professionals, but to the care, humility, and accuracy with which professional practitioners craft and interpret their work.[30] Responsibility dictates that: *No political inquiry of any kind should claim a rigor or scientific capacity that it does not possess nor should it facilitate, or neglect the prevention of, misinterpretations concerning its rigor and scientific capacity, no matter what it demands of opposing ideas or other scholarship.*

Responsibility is not limited to the written word, but applies to all instances where the political scientist acts as the producer, purveyor, or interpreter of political "knowledge." If within the context of the consultant or expert role he "sells" to consumers as established knowledge something that is not established knowledge at all but, rather, speculation or a quantified model, then he is acting irresponsibly. If in the face of grandiose expectations held by consumers he nurtures their delusions through his professional repute (though the necessary knowledge is nonexistent) or if he palms off whatever he has in his bag without giving proper warning of its limitations or of its divergence from what the consumers are looking for, then he is acting irresponsibly.

In substantive inquiry, responsibility dictates much more than rhetorical humility or the skillfull use of caveats. It charges researchers and theorists with the task of accurately meshing claims or conclusions with the logical warrant provided by the methodological and epistemological basis of the particular inquiry.[31] In broad assessments of the profession's evolution and capacity, responsibility precludes the "oversell" of political science or its knowledge through exaggerated claims concerning service functions or epistemological rigor and reliability.[32]

A Normative Paradigm for Responsible Scholarship[33]

What follows does not constitute a code of ethics but, rather, a framework within which ethical problems might be approached. The crux of evaluating the responsibility of scholarship is to determine what is being asserted.

1. *What empirical, theoretiral, or normative claims and contentions are being advanced by the scholarship in question?*

Determining fairly and accurately what is being offered or claimed is what renders the notion of responsibility an analytic rather than ideological gestalt. Any scholarship can be condemned or praised to suit the ideological whims or cathartic urge of the reviewer without his grasping what is actually offered. Item 1 demands that scholarship be judged on its own merits. In most instances, the nebulous nature of claims, the skillful use of caveats, and the complexity of purpose make it extremely difficult to determine in a fair and lucid manner what is actually being put forth. The perspective of analysis for Item 1 is not how well claims are substantiated or what implicit contentions the reviewer can illumniate; it is what claims the scholarship itself explicitly makes. At this point, the reviewer takes the scholarship at face value and merely catalogues its major contentions.

2. *What is the nature, quantity, and quality of that which the scholarship in question specifically employs to support its claims and contentions?*

This is not an appraisal of how well the case is made. It is a cataloguing of the character, capacity, and number of sources used to support the claims and contentions discovered under Item 1. More central considerations relating to Item 2 are:

Is empirical evidence offered as support?

How many types of empirical evidence are offered and what is their nature?

How valid and well constructed does each appear to be?

The last question deals with the quality of the empirical sup-

port offered, as measured against the labels given it in the scholarship under scrutiny. That is, how good is it, given the kind of
empiricism it is purported to be? If it is designated by the producers
of the scholarship as "survey research," or if lacking any designation by the producers it is best described as such, what sampling
techniques are used? If the empiricism is a classificatory schema,
how precise are the criteria and concepts used in classification?
If it employs game theory, what assumptions about reality does
it make, and how do these compare with standard modes of game
theory?

3. *What links does the scholarship in question offer between its
supportive evidence and its claims and contentions?*

The task here is to map out the links of argument as they are
presented by the author(s), not as they are evaluated by the
reviewer. If empirical support is offered, what are its stated links to
various contentions? Is the evidence asserted to support conclusively all of the major contentions, some of them, or none of
them?

4. *Considering the scope, character, and derivation of claims
and contentions, the scope, nature, and quality of supportive evidence, and the purported links between the two, is the scholarship in question responsible?*

It is here that normative judgment is exercised, building upon
the preceding analysis. Irresponsibility is directly proportional to
the gap between what is claimed and what is provided. It varies
also with the nature of the gap and with the manner by which
it is concealed or the degree of ignorance and carelessness that
it manifests. Normative condemnations of irresponsibility must
be devoid of considerations of conspiracy, personal motive, or
ideological consequences; they must not be derived from invective
or professional factionalism, but from logical criteria applied
analytically; they concern only professional competence and the
internal validity of scholarship. The frame of reference for Item
4 is not logical positivism or behavioralism per se. It is, instead,
what the scholarship in question actually does, compared with what
it purports to do, on the basis of what we know about the nature

and limits of various modes of political analysis and various kinds of supportive evidence.

The universe of normative judgments about responsibility (and their quality) thus varies according to the profession's ability to employ analytical skills and to assess the epistemological state of the art. The less political science knows about its "scientific" capacity and about the logic of inquiry, the less it can accurately judge responsibility. In seeking to be responsible, the profession can gain a greater sense of its limits, potentials, and ethical dynamics. It is not necessary—or even desirable—that the notion of responsibility evolves into a detailed ethical code, but only that the profession seeks to cultivate and assess responsibility.

Toward Responsibility: The Role of Professional Culture[34]

The following goals for (or reorientations of) professional culture would facilitate a more responsible climate for political inquiry. It is not claimed that the suggestions are exhaustive or that their realization would constitute the ethical millennium. Still, as a learned community, political science might pursue these and other avenues of creating a more responsible professionalism.

MORE EDUCATION; LESS SOCIALIZATION

Curricula, especially at the graduate level where professional socialization takes place, should give more attention to cultivating the ability to evaluate the limits and capacities of "knowledge," its epistemic and existential bases, and its value and policy consequences. When socialization to mainstream approaches and techniques occurs in relative or absolute isolation from such concerns, it becomes one-dimensional. It may then result in a trained incapacity to evaluate meaningfully one's own work and that of his profession. This analytical incapacity tends to foster either an indiscriminate allegiance to or a blanket rejection of the profession's mainstream scholarship, rooted in ideological or value preferences rather than analytical judgment.

VIABLE INTELLECTUAL PLURALISM

A viable intellectual pluralism is not necessarily provided by the profession's tendency toward a schizoid identification with the powerful and the powerless. Ideological balance or confrontation within the profession need not provide intellectual pluralism, and is certainly not synonymous with it. Nor is the recruitment of minority persons necessarily productive of intellectual pluralism, regardless of whether such groups are racially, economically, or politically defined. It may only broaden the demographic base of professional culture—and possibly its substance—without ameliorating its trained incapacities. In terms of professional dynamics, the degree of education versus socialization is more important to intellectual pluralism than are recruitment patterns.

Enhancing intellectual pluralism may require that the priorities and tendencies of professionalism be tempered in behalf of the freedom from orthodoxy which pursuit of science and knowledge demands. If there exists a genuine commitment to intellectual pluralism, with all the ambiguities of that term, then the American Political Science Association Council should give primary attention to the cultivation and articulation of diverse intellectual interests within the professional role of political scientist. Only an active commitment by the Association itself can curb the orthodox tendencies inherent in professional organization.

This role should not be predominantly redistributive: redistributing professional resources and rewards to the profession's have-nots, however they may be defined. But it should seek to nourish important intellectual functions which might atrophy unless actively sustained. Sustenance may be in the form of exhortations, resources, or opportunities. Areas of intellectual endeavor which might currently need attention are: a) epistemological analysis of various modes and techniques of inquiry; b) the development of skills, concepts, and approaches for quality teaching at both graduate and undergraduate levels; and c) normative discourse on politics and human values.

A Commitment to Introspection

The American Political Science Association should channel more of its resources toward a penetrating examination of its professional processes and milieu, rather than allowing itself to become fixated with welfare and repute functions. A commitment to introspection, coupled with a viable intellectual pluralism, can strengthen resistance to orthodoxy and to a public policy role of expost facto legitimation. Analytical introspection, not synonymous with criticism of dominant professional values, is the key to responsible professionalism.

Reevaluating the Problems of Professional Ethics

The Association's Committee on Professional Ethics might examine the complex problems of responsible professionalism and work to create a climate of scholarly responsibility which abjures inflated claims of theoretical or manipulative capacity. Surely some kind of epistemic categorical imperative urging that "one claim no more for one's work, however circumspectly, than is demonstrably inherent in it" would be as viable and important as the committee's statements on the ethics of funding, teacher-student relationships, and manuscript submissions.

The attainment of a responsible professional culture will not guarantee a science of politics, but it will lead political science away from pseudoscience. It may not sanctify the profession's policy involvements, but it will reduce the potential for symbolic manipulations of expertise. It will not render inquiry value free, but it will help the profession to discern the epistemological value of its knowledge. Though its thrust is epistemological, the concept of responsibility offered here avoids canonical rigidity and attempts to be cognizant of both the complex nature of ethical problems and the evolutionary nature of political inquiry within the knowledgeable society.

References

CHAPTER II

1. Robert E. Lane, "The Decline of Politics and Ideology in a Knowledgeable Society," *The American Sociological Review*, 31 (October, 1966), 649-662; at 650.

2. Alexis de Tocqueville, *Democracy in America*, ed. Richard D. Heffner (New York: The New American Library, 1956). Lane, *op. cit.*, pp. 653-657, describes "thoughtways" as the characteristic thought patterns and emphases of the knowledgeable society. Two such thought patterns are "employment of objective truth criteria" and "tolerance of dissonance and ambiguity."

3. For an analysis of the influence of abundance upon American character, see David M. Potter, *People of Plenty* (Chicago: University of Chicago Press, 1954).

4. Thomas Molnar, *The Decline of the Intellectual* (New York: World Publishing Co., 1961), chap. 9.

5. Tocqueville, *op. cit.*, pp. 156-158, on perfectibility; and Molnar, *op. cit.*, chaps. 6 and 9, on perceptions of knowledge and environment.

6. Spencer Klaw, *The New Brahmins* (New York: Wm. Morrow & Co., 1968), p. 12.

7. See Molnar, *op. cit.*, chap. 9, on progressivism and utopianism in American intellectual thought.

8. Don K. Price, *The Scientific Estate* (New York: Oxford University Press, 1965).

9. Klaw, *loc. cit.*

10. Charles H. Backstrom, "The Social Scientist As Policy Maker or The Astigmatic Leading the Blind and Vice Versa," paper presented at the 1961 American Political Science Association annual meeting, St. Louis, Sept. 6-9. Reprinted in *The Use of Social Research in Federal Domestic Programs*, III, Committee on Government Operations (Washington: Government Printing Office, 1967), 232.

11. Everrett C. Ladd, *American Political Parties: Social Change and Political Response* (New York: W. W. Norton, 1970), p. 262.

12. The concept of the "knowledge market" appears in Fritz Machlup, *The Production and Distribution of Knowledge in the United States* (Princeton: Princeton University Press, 1962).

13. A more detailed analysis of modern trends in the American university appears in the next chapter.

14. Lane, *op. cit.*, p. 662.

15. Robert S. Lynd, *Knowledge For What?* (Princeton: Princeton University Press, 1939).

16. The sociology of knowledge applied to political science will be a

major concern of succeeding chapters (especially Ch. V). A classic statement of a general nature is Karl Mannheim, *Ideology and Utopia: An Introduction to the Sociology of Knowledge* (New York: Harcourt Brace, 1936).

17. Descriptions of both personal influence and interest group competition possess insights for the understanding of internal and external professional dynamics, a large part of which may be usefully analyzed as "occupational politics." See David B. Truman, *The Governmental Process* (New York: Knopf, 1951); Elihu Katz and Paul F. Lazarsfeld, *Personal Influence* (New York: The Free Press, 1955).

18. Edgar Litt, *The Public Vocational University: Captive Knowledge and Public Power* (New York: Holt, Rinehart, and Winston, 1969), p. 8. Tensions of this type, within political science, are posited by Bertrand de Jeuvenal, "On the Nature of Political Science," *American Political Science Review*, 55, no. 4 (December, 1961), 773-779.

19. Anthony Downs, "A Realistic Look at the Final Payoffs of Urban Data Systems," *Public Administration Review*, XXVII, no. 3 (September, 1967), 204-210.

20. Edward Shils, "Privacy and Power," in Ithiel de Sola Pool (ed.), *Contemporary Political Science* (New York: McGraw-Hill, 1967), pp. 231-276.

21. Aaron Wildavsky, "Practical Consequences of the Theoretical Study of Defense Policy," *Public Administration Review*, 25 (March, 1965), 91-103. Wildawsky describes the use of intellectual expertise as a primary style of policy decision making in an increasing number of policy areas. See also Harold L. Wilensky, *Organizational Intelligence: Knowledge and Government and Industry* (New York: Basic Books, 1967).

22. See Ernest Nagel, *The Structure of Science* (New York: Harcourt Brace & World, Inc., 1961), pp. 485-502.

CHAPTER III

1. Robert K. Merton, *Social Theory and Social Structure* (Glencoe, Ill.: The Free Press, 1968 enlarged edition), pp. 514-516.

2. Anselm L. Strauss and Lee Rainwater, *The Professional Scientist: A Study of the American Chemist* (Chicago: Aldine Pub. Co., 1962), pp. 4-10.

3. Everett C. Hughes, *Men and Their Work* (Glencoe, Ill.: The Free Press, 1958), pp. 80-82.

4. *Ibid.*, pp. 139-142.

5. David Reisman and Christopher Jencks, *The Academic Revolution* (New York: Doubleday, Inc., 1967), p. 23. This theme appears throughout the book, but is heavily emphasized in the chapters dealing directly with professionalism.

6. David Reisman, *Constraint and Variety in American Education* (New York: Doubleday, Inc., 1968), pp. 101-106.

7. William Graham Summer, *Folkways* (Boston: Ginn & Co., 1906), sections 40, 41, 56, 61, an 63.

8. C. Wright Mills, *White Collar* (New York: Oxford University Press, 1951), chap. 11.

9. This point is expounded in various organizational contexts in: Herbert A. Simon, Donald W. Smithburg, and Victor Thompson, *Public Administration* (New York: Alfred A. Knopf, Inc., 1964); Robert Presthus, *The Organizational Society* (New York: Alfred A. Knopf, Inc., 1965); Victor Thompson, *Modern Organization* (New York: Alfred A. Knopf, Inc., 1961).

10. Presthus, *op. cit.*, pp. 140-141.

11. Strauss and Rainwater, *op. cit.*, pp. 145-170, 213.

12. Scott A. Greer, *Social Organization* (New York: Random House, 1955), p. 22.

13. Roger Brown, *Social Psychology* (New York: The Free Press, 1965), p. 156.

14. Strauss and Rainwater, *op. cit.*, chap. 8.

15. Brown, *op. cit.*, p. 155.   16. *Ibid.*, chap. 11.

17. See discussions of organizational conflicts generated by the professional role in Thompson, *loc. cit.;* Mark Abrahamson (ed.), *The Professional in the Organization* (Chicago: Rand McNally, 1967).

18. Neil H. Cheek, Jr., "The Social Role of the Professional," in Abrahamson, *op. cit.*, pp. 9-16.

19. See Norwood Russell Hanson, *Patterns of Discovery* (Cambridge, Eng.: University Press, 1958), chaps. 1-4.

20. Elvi Whittaker and Virginia Olson, "The Faces of Florence Nightingale: Functions of the Heroine Legend in an Occupational Sub-Culture," *Human Organization,* XIII, no. 2 (Summer, 1964), pp. 123-130.

21. Mills, *loc. cit.*

22. The characteristics of bureaucracy are depicted in Max Weber, *From Max Weber,* ed. and trans. H. H. Gerth and C. Wright Mills (New York: Oxford University Press, 1958), pp. 196-198.

23. Reisman and Jencks, *op. cit.*   24. *Ibid.*, p. 201.

25. Mills, *op. cit.*, pp. 133-137; C Wright Mills, *The Sociological Imagination* (New York: Oxford University Press, 1959).

26. Strauss and Rainwater, *op. cit.*, pp. 76-79, 219, found considerable mobility in the chemistry profession, where shifts of occupational locus among government, industry, and academia were frequent.

27. A contrast to this ethos is provided by Jacques Barzun, *The American University* (New York: Harper & Row, 1968).

28. Fritz Machlup, *The Production and Distribution of Knowledge in the United States* (Princeton: Princeton University Press, 1962).

29. Clark Kerr, *The Uses of the University* (Cambridge: Harvard University Press, 1963), chap. 1.

CAPTER IV

1. Albert Somit and Joseph Tanenhaus, *American Political Science: A Profile of a Discipline* (New York: Prentice-Hall, 1964). This study documents the membership's perceptions of outstanding scholars and works; a good deal of agreement was evidenced.

2. James March and Heinz Eulau (eds.), *Political Science* (Englewood Cliffs, N.J.: Prentice-Hall, 1969), p. 68. The 1970 figure was obtained from the *Program*, 1970 American Political Science Association Annual Meeting, p. 154; 1973 from *PS*, VI, no. 3 (Summer, 1973), 309; 1974 from PS, VII, no 3 (Summer, 1974), 287. Institutional memberships, which comprise, about a quarter of each yearly total, are lumped with individual ones because both provide evidence of professional growth.

3. *Program*, op. cit., p. 81.

4. Thomas E. Mann, "Report On A Survey," *PS*, no. 4 (Fall 1974), p. 382.

5. *Ibid*

6. See Alan Wolfe, "Practicing the Pluralism We Preach: The Internal Process of the American Political Science Association," *Antioch Review*, 29 no. 3 (Fall, 1969), 353-374; Albert Somit and Joseph Tanenhaus, *The Development of American Political Science* (Boston: Allyn and Bacon, Inc., 1967), p. 155.

7. The prestige ratings were those of Allan M. Cartter, *An Assessment of Quality in Graduate Education* (Washington, D.C.: American Council on Education, 1966). Doctoral output statistics appear in Somit and Tanenhaus, *The Development of American Political Science*, p. 165.

8. Somit and Tanenhaus, *American Political Science*, p. 79.

9. The cumulative character of prestige is described in Wolfe, *op. cit.*

10. "Profile of Ph.D. Recipients in Political Science in 1968," *PS*, II, no. 4 (Fall, 1969), p. 659.

11. William Buchanan, "The Market for Doctoral Instruction in Political Science," paper presented at the 1967 American Political Science Association Annual Meeting, Chicago.

12. "Profile of Ph.D. Recipients in Political Science in 1968," *loc. cit.*

13. "Assessing Candidates for Graduate Study in Political Science," *PS*, II, no. 4 (Fall, 1969), pp. 612-613.

14. Somit and Tanenhaus, *The Development of American Political Science*, p. 33.

15. *Ibid.*, pp. 33-34.   16. March and Eulau, *op. cit.*, p. 119.

17. "Obstacles to Graduate Education in Political Science," *PS*, II, no. 4 (Fall, 1969), pp. 630-641, at 632.

18. *Ibid.*, p. 631.   19. *Ibid.*, p. 635.

20. Somit and Tanenhaus, *The Development of American Political Science*, p. 54.

21. Mann, *op. cit.*, p. 385.

22. "Report of the Executive Director" (American Political Science Association, 1965-1966), p. 53.

23. March and Eulau, *op. cit.*, p. 86.   24. *Ibid.*, pp. 88-89.

25. Somit and Tanenhaus, *The Development of American Political Science*, p. 167.

26. See *ibid.*, pp. 167-168. Prestige ratings are those of Cartter, *op. cit.*

27. March and Eulau, *op. cit.*, pp. 86-87.

28. *Ibid.*, p. 99.   29 *Ibid*, pp. 100-102.

30. Taken from "Report of the Treasurer 1973-4," *PS*, VI, no. 3 (Summer, 1974), p. 290.

31. "APSA Investments and Securities," *PS*, III, no. 2 (Spring, 1970), p. 209.

32. March and Eulau, *op. cit.*, p. 132.

33. For example, of 924 articles published in three of the most prestigious journals between 1959 and 1969, only one dealt with Vietnam, thirteen with racial politics, five with urban politics, twelve with foreign and defense policies, and thirty-four were general treatises on public policy. Thus, 6 per cent of all articles surveyed dealt with policy analysis in the broadest terms, about 3 per cent with concrete domestic or foreign policies, and about 3 per cent with general analysis of methodology. The journals were *The American Political Science Review, The Political Science Quarterly*, and *The Journal of Politics*. Their high repute among political scientists is documented in Somit and Tanenhaus, *American Political Science*, pp. 190-192.

34. Mann, *op. cit.*, p. 383.

35. "Statement of Intent," *PS*, III, no 2 (Spring, 1970), p. 97.

36. Somit and Tanenhaus, *The Development of American Political Science*, p. 155.

37. *Ibid.*   38. *Ibid.*, pp. 149-150.

39. See *PS*, VI, no. 3 (Summer, 1973), pp. 315-316, 340-341.

CHAPTER V

1. A good survey of the literature is provided in James E. Curtis and John W. Petras (eds.), *The Sociology of Knowledge* (New York: Praeger Publishers, 1970). The application of the sociology of knowledge to the profession as described in this chapter appears in capsulized form in "Bringing The Sociology of Knowledge To Bear On Political Science," *Polity*, Summer, 1975.

2. This is discussed in Philip H. Melanson, "The Political Science Profession, Political Knowledge and Public Policy," *Politics and Society*, 2, no. 4 (Summer, 1972), pp. 489-501.

3. Karl Mannheim, *Ideology and Utopia: An Introduction to the Sociology of Knowledge*, trans. Louis Worth and Edward Shils (New York: Harvest Books, 1936). See also William E. Connolly's application of Mannheim to political science: *Political Science and Ideology* (New York: Antherton Press, 1967).

4. Mannheim, *op. cit.*; H. H. Gerth and C. Wright Mills (eds.), *From*

Max Weber (New York: Oxford University Press, 1958); C. Wright Mills, *The Sociological Imagination* (New York: Oxford University Press, 1959); Robert K. Merton, *Social Theory and Social Structure* (Glencoe, Ill.: The Free Press, 1968 enlarged edition).

5. Ernest Grünwald, "The Sociology of Knowledge and Epistemology," trans. Rainer Koehne, in Curtis and Petras, *op. cit.*, pp. 237-243, at p. 237.

6. A. R. Louch, *Explanation and Human Action* (Berkeley: University of California Press, 1966), p. 207.

7. Grünwald, *op., cit.*, p. 238.

8. Scientific consciousness in this context does not necessarily refer to a rigid, deductive kind of formulation, but, as James N. Rosenau describes, the kind of inquiry where errors cannot be ignored, where explanations are cast in if-then terms, and where the conditions under which the postulations could be shown right or wrong are made explicit. A scientific consciousness fosters an orientation that sets out to explain certain phenomena, or to define them strictly, order and classify them, and then relate them logically to other data and other logical explanatory structures. It is, as Ernest Nagel describes, a perspective that seeks to "discover and formulate in general terms the conditions under which events of various sorts occur, the statements of such determining conditions being the explanations of corresponding happenings. This goal can only be achieved by distinguishing and isolating certain properties in the subject matter studied and by ascertaining the repeatable patterns of dependence in which the properties stand to one another." The concept of scientific consciousness is taken from James N. Rosenau, "Moral Fervor, Systematic Analysis, and Scientific Consciousness in Foreign Policy Research," Austin Ranney (ed.), *Political Science and Public Policy* (Chicago: Markham Publishing Co., 1968), p. 211; Ernest Nagel, *The Structure of Science* (New York: Harcourt Brace and World, 1961), p. 4.

9. The concept of the "confessional" is taken from Paul F. Kress, "On Locating Partitions: George Devereau's Contributions to the Methodology of Behavioral Science," paper presented at the annual meeting of the American Political Science Association, Los Angeles, September 8-12, 1970.

10. *Ibid.*, p. 12.

11. See Karl Popper, "The Sociology of Knowledge," in Curtis and Petras, *op. cit.*, pp. 649-660.

12. Peter L. Berger and Thomas Luckman, *The Social Construction of Reality* (New York: Doubleday, 1966). The authors exclude epistemological concerns, but broaden the definition of the sociology of knowledge. Note especially the introduction.

13. *Ibid.*, p. 3.

14. Problems of scientific philosophy relating to political inquiry are discussed in "Symposium on Scientific Explanation in Political Science," *American Political Science Review*, LXIII, no. 4 (December, 1969), pp. 1233-1262.

15. See Charles A. McCoy and John Playford (eds.) *Apolitical*

Politics: A Critique of Behavioralism (New York: Thomas Y. Crowell Co., 1967).

16. Various aspects of the profession's collective value biases are discussed in Lewis Lipsitz, "Vulture, Mantis, and Seal," *Polity*, III, no. 1 (Fall, 1970), 3-21; McCoy and Playford, *op. cit.;* Edgar Litt and Philip H. Melanson, "A Peer Group of Liberals: The Profession and Its Public Discontents," paper presented at the annual meeting of the American Political Science Association, New York, 1969.

17. Popper, *op. cit.*, pp. 645-657.

18. The purpose of offering the following examples is not to denigrate the scholarly worth of the books and articles that are criticized, but to illustrate the necessity of applying the sociology of knowledge to political inquiry. The examples are posited to be typical of the kinds of biases that plague much of the profession's research in a variety of substantive areas. The analysis of these examples takes its inspiration from Robert K. Merton's "paradigm for the sociology of knowledge," though this paradigm is not expressly applied. See Merton, *op. cit.*, pp. 460-488.

19. The epistemological goals of the behavioral revolution in political science are elaborated in David Easton, *The Political System* (New York: Alfred A. Knopf, 1953), chap. 2. Biases of the kind about to be illustrated preclude the attainment of what Easton describes as reliable knowledge. See Melanson, *op. cit.*

20. See N. R. Hanson, *Patterns of Discovery* (Cambridge, Eng.: University Press, 1961), chaps. I-IV; F. S. C. Northrop, *The Logic of the Sciences and Humanities* (New York: The Macmillan Co., 1947), pp. 19-35, 77-101.

21. William E. Connolly (ed.), *The Bias of Pluralism* (New York: Atherton Press, 1969), pp. 22-24.

22. *Ibid.*

23. Primary examples of works evidencing assumptions of sequential development include C. E. Black, *The Dynamics of Modernization* (New York: Harper and Brothers, 1966); A. F. K. Organski, *The Stages of Political Development* (New York: Alfred A. Knopf, 1965); Walt W. Rostow. *The Stages of Economic Growth* (Cambridge: M.I.T. Press, 1960); Gerhard E. Lenski, *Power and Privilege: A Theory of Social Stratification* (New York: The Free Press, 1960). Sequential assumptions are implicit in "stage" theories of development.

24. John D. Montgomery, "The Quest for Political Development," *Comparative Politics*, 1, no. 2 (January, 1969), 289. Pervasive notions of unilinear or patterned development increasingly like Western democracy may be tied to the doctrine of progress that is so prominent in the Western and American intellectual traditions. See Ali Mazuri, "From Social Darwinism to Theories of Modernization: A Tradition of Analysis," *World Politics*, 21, no. 1 (October, 1968), pp. 69-85.

25. Philip H. Melanson and Lauriston R. King, "Theory in Comparative Politics: A Critical Appraisal," *Comparative Political Studies*, 4, no. 2 (July, 1971), 205-231.

26. See G. Lowell Field, *Comparative Political Development: The*

162   POLITICAL SCIENCE AND POLITICAL KNOWLEDGE

Precedent of the West (Ithaca: Cornell University Press, 1967), chap. I.

27. Examples of this tendency to focus on "democracy" as a key variable include S. M. Lipset, "Some Social Requisites of Democracy: Economic Development and Political Legitimacy," *American Political Science Review,* 53 (1959), 69-106; L. W. Shannon, "Is Level of Development Related to Capacity for Self-Government?" *American Journal of Economics and Sociology,* 17 (1958), 367-381; and "Socio-Economic Development and Political Status," *Social Problems,* 7 (1959), 157-169; Philips Cutright, "National Political Development: Measurement and Analysis," *American Sociological Review,* 28 (1963), 253-254; Donald J. McCrone and Charles F. Cnudde, "Toward a Communication Theory of Democratic Political Development," *American Political Science Review,* 61 (1967), 72-79.

28. Melanson and King, *op. cit.*

29. See note 4. These works elaborate upon the mental bonds of cultural milieu.

30. Elliot S. White, "Intelligence and Sense of Political Efficacy in Children," *Journal of Politics,* 30, no. 3 (August, 1968), 710-731.

31. See K. Elles *et al., Intelligence and Cultural Difference* (Chicago: University of Chicago Press, 1951).

32. Another example of the failure to control for middle-class bias and the authority structure of the school environment is David Easton and Jack Dennis, "A Child's Acquisition of Regime Norms; Political Efficacy," *American Political Science Review,* 61, no. 1 (March, 1967), 25-38.

33. Roberta Segal, "Image of a President: Some Insights into the Political Views of School Children," Research Note, *American Political Science Review,* 62, no. 1 (March, 1968), 216.

34. Dean Jaros, Herbert Hirch, and Frederick Fleron, "The Malevolent Leader; Political Socialization in an American Sub-Culture," *American Political Science Review,* 62, no. 2, (June, 1968), 564-575. These "malevolent" perceptions were in sharp contrast to the "benevolent" ones found by Fred I. Greenstein, "The Benevolent Leader: Children's Images of Political Authority," *American Political Science Review,* 56, no. 4 (December, 1960), 934-943.

35. The assumptions and contentions of socialization theory in political science vis-à-vis political culture are elaborated in Gabriel A. Almond and Sidney Verba, *The Civic Culture* (Princeton: Princeton University Press, 1963). A survey of much of the socialization research inside and outside political science is provided by Richard E. Dawson and Kenneth Prewitt, *Political Socialization* (Boston: Little, Brown and Co., 1969).

36. The term "logical warrant" is put forth by Norton Long in Eugene Meehan, *Explanation in the Social Sciences: A System Paradigm* (Homewood, Ill.: The Dorsey Press, 1968), Foreword, p. vi.

37. Almond and Verba, *op. cit.*

38. This analysis is taken from Melanson and King, *op. cit.*

39. Almond and Verba, *op. cit.*

40. *Ibid.,* p. 8.

41. Gabriel A. Almond and G. Bingham Powell, *Comparative Politics: A Developmental Approach* (Boston: Little Brown and Co., 1966). The analysis of this book is taken from Melanson and King, *op. cit.*

42. Almond and Powell, *op. cit.*, pp. 322-323.

43. *Ibid.*, p. 323.

44. Some examples of varying expositions of this theme are: Connolly, *op. cit.*; Charles A. McCoy and John Playford (eds.), *Apolitical Politics: A Critique of Behavioralism* (New York: Thomas Y. Crowell Co., 1967); Henry S. Kariel, "Expanding the Political Present," *American Political Science Review*, 63, no. 3 (September, 1969), 768-776.

45. These pressures are generated by the profession itself, by the institutions in which political scientists work, and by the cost-benefit, consumer-producer dynamics of what is aptly described as the "knowledge market." Professional pressures to publish and research are described in Albert Somit and Joseph Tanenhaus, *American Political Science: Profile of a Discipline* (New York: Atherton Press, 1964). Institutional pressures are described in Robert Presthus, *The Organizational Society* (New York: Knopf, Inc., 1965); Edgar Litt, *The Public Vocational University* (New York: Holt, Rinehart and Winston, 1969). The pressures of the knowledge market are discussed in Fritz Machlup, *The Production and Distribution of Knowledge in America* (Princeton: Princeton University Press, 1962).

CHAPTER VI: PART I

1. The term "grand theory" was coined by C. Wright Mills to describe vague abstractions that are so nebulous that they preclude verification. See *The Sociological Imagination* (New York: Oxford University Press, 1959), chap. 2.

2. Martin Landau, "Comment: On Objectivity," *American Political Science Review*, 66, no. 3 (September, 1972), 853.

3. The notion of "craftsmanship" draws its inspiration from Mills' discussion of "intellectual craftsmanship": Mills, *op. cit.*, pp. 195-226.

4. Bertrand de Jeuvenal argues that the fear of knowing certain things that might be detrimental to dominant values has significantly influenced the intellectual evolution of political science: "On the Nature of Political Science," *American Political Science Review*, 55, no. 4 (December, 1961) 773-779.

5. At this point, the exhortations for epistemic craftsmanship sound much like Easton's plea for a more scientific study of politics: *The Political System* (New York: Alfred A. Knopf, 1953), chap. 2. But Easton did not, in this work, escape the realm of grand theory. In contrast, this chapter will attempt to say something more concrete about the problems of explanation in political science.

6. A survey of these arguments appears in Martin Landau, *Political Theory and Political Science* (New York: Macmillan Co., 1972), chap. I.

7. Ernest Nagel, *The Structure of Science* (New York: Harcourt Brace & World, 1961), pp. 485-502.

8. *Ibid.,* pp. 473-485.

9. A discussion of this issue appears in David Braybrooke (ed.), *Philosophical Problems of the Social Sciences* (New York: Macmillan Co., 1965). The "outside view is expounded by B. F. Skinner, "The Scheme of Behavior Explanation," pp. 42-52; the "inside" view is advocated by Alfred Schutz, "The Theory of Social Action," pp. 53-67.

10. John G. Gunnell, "The Idea of Conceptual Framework: A Philosophical Critique," *Journal of Comparative Administration,* 1, no. 1 (August, 1969), 140-176.

11. Examples of this literature are cited throughout this chapter, especially in the section dealing specifically with "explanation."

12. A debate about the assets and liabilities of the hypothetico-deductive method of explanation appears in: "Symposium on Scientific Explanation in Political Science," *American Political Science Review,* 63, no. 4 (December, 1969), 1233-1262.

13. Eugene Meehan, *Explanation in the Social Sciences: A System Paradigm* (Homewood, Ill.: Dorsey Press, 1968). This attempt to develop a form of explanation suited for social science escapes the models of established science but fails to come up with a viable replacement. Meehan approaches the problem from a definitional perspective, and while redefining "explanation," he neglects to deal effectively with the validity of knowledge. In fact, he opens the way to even more confusion than now exists by purposely separating the empirical and logical aspects of "explanation." He sees this as a pragmatic step toward useful knowledge. But his overemphasis upon problems of method and of the scope of inquiry precipitates a neglect of the more basic problem of how to recognize valid knowledge. This is the epistemic price paid for achieving flexibility by compartmentalizing (or, in effect, legislating out) the logical aspects of explanation. Moreover, Meehan's new flexibility "attaches no weight to the purposes for which explanations are sought or to the manner in which they are used" (p. 10). Thus the role of political knowledge in the knowledgeable society is excluded. Exempting these concerns and divorcing logic from empiricism goes far beyond the realm of pragmatic flexibility. Instead, it begs some of the most important questions concerning explanation in social science.

14. Easton, *loc. cit.*

15. David Easton, *A Framework for Political Analysis* (Englewood Cliffs, N.J.: Prentice-Hall, 1965); Mills, *op. cit.,* p. 13.

16. See "Symposium on Scientific Explanation in Political Science," *op. cit.*

17. *Ibid.*

18. The contention is not that theoretical refinement renders knowledge totally "objective" or value free, but only that it reduces, to some degree, the latitude for both logical interpretation and crass manipulation of findings.

19. Hans Reichenbach, *The Rise of Scientific Philosophy* (Berkeley: University of California Press, 1951).

20. *Ibid.*, pp. 1-50.

21. See Eugene F. Miller, "Positivism, Historicism, and Political Inquiry," *American Political Science Review*, 66, no. 3 (September, 1972), 796.

22. Gunnell, *loc. cit.*; Gunnell, "Deduction, Explanation, and Social Scientific Inquiry," "Symposium on Scientific Explanation in Political Science," *op. cit.*, pp. 1233-1246.

23. A good example of the theoretical poverty of much hypothesization in political science appears in Gabriel A. Almond and G. Bingham Powell, *Comparative Politics: A Developmental Approach* (Boston: Little Brown and Co., 1966). After hundreds of pages of regime descriptions and classifications, the authors say: "The basic theoretical statement here is that the development of higher levels of system capabilities is dependent upon the development of greater structural differentiation and cultural secularization," p. 323.

Because they use definitions and indices of "system capabilities" that are drawn from general notions of modernization (and democracy), the link to "secularization" and "structural differentiation" (two of the most pervasive, visible, and understood characteristics of modernity) renders their "theoretical statement" tautological. The empirical congruence of modernity and democracy further exacerbates the circularity of this proposition. See Almond and Powell's discussion, pp. 190-212.

24. This term is used by Rudolf Carnap, who is one of the founders of the logical positivist school: *The Logical Structure of the World,* trans. Rolf A. George (Berkeley: University of California Press, 1967). Exposition of the epistemological foundations of logical positivism are found in Moritz Schlick, *Allgemeine Erkenntnislehre* (Berlin: J. Springer, 1918); A. J. Ayer, "Introduction" to *Logical Positivism* (Glencoe, Ill.: The Free Press, 1959); Peter Achinstein and Stephen F. Barker (eds.), *The Legacy of Logical Positivism* (Baltimore: Johns Hopkins Press, 1969).

25. The extreme fixation for gathering data and the neglect of larger theoretical concerns that have characterized empiricism in political science are termed "hyperfactualism" by Easton, *The Political System*, chap. 2. The notions that data accretion is inherently scientific and that the sheer quantity of data accreted will help the discipline conceptually are still very prominent. Inductive notions of this type appear in Karl W. Deutsch, "The Theoretical Basis of Data Programs," in Richard L. Merritt and Stein Rokan (eds.), *Comparing Nations* (New Haven: Yale University Press, 1966), pp. 27-56; Ralph Braibanti, "Comparative Political Analytics Reconsidered," *Journal of Politics*, 30, no. 1 (February, 1968), 25-65.

26. The term "abstracted empiricism" appears in Mills, *op. cit.*, chap. 3. The term is a pejorative one referring to fixations for data collection that lack a sense of what needs to be known.

27. This problem is discussed in David Braybrooke and Alexander Rosenberg, "Comment: Getting the War News Straight: The Actual Situation in the Philosophy of Science," *American Political Science Re-*

view, 66, no. 3 (September, 1972), 818-826, at 821, 826.

28. Norwood Russell Hanson, *Patterns of Discovery* (Cambridge, Eng.: Cambridge University Press, 1958), p. 64.

29. *Ibid.;* Thomas Kuhn, *The Structure of Scientific Revolutions* (Chicago: University of Chicago Press, 1962); Kenneth F. Schaffner, "Correspondence Rules," *Philosophy of Science*, 36, no. 3 (September, 1969), 280-290. Schaffner supports this viewpoint through his examination of correspondence rules. This perspective on scientific development is central to the "revolt" against positivism within the philosophy of science and is a primary theme of the works of such scholars as Stephen Toulmin, Michael Scriven, Norwood R. Hanson, Paul Feyerabend, and Peter Winch. This approach is often labeled "descriptive" or "contextualist." It attacks not only inductive, incremental interpretations of scientific development and logical positivist tenets, but also the rigidities of the "deductive model" of explanation, on the grounds that it does not reflect the character of scientific explanation.

30. Mills, *op. cit.*, chaps. 2 and 3.   31. *Ibid.*, p. 125.

32. Of course, there is always a positive role for epistemic craftsmanship as well as a preventive one. In this case, the positive role is to render the descriptions and monographs as competent, productive, and systematic as possible.

33. Eugene Meehan, *Contemporary Political Thought* (Homewood, Ill.: Dorsey Press, 1967), pp. 23-26.

34. F. S. C. Northrop, *The Logic of the Sciences and Humanities* (New York: Macmillan Co., 1947), chaps. 1-4.

35. Charles E. Woodson, "Parameter Estimation Vs. Hypothesis Testing," *Philosophy of Science*, 36, no. 2 (June, 1969), 203-204.

36. Paul E. Meehl, "Theory Testing in Psychology and Physics: A Methodological Paradox," *Philosophy of Science*, 34, no. 2 (June, 1967), 103-115, quotations at p. 103.

37. David C. Leege, "On Measurement of Dependent Variables in Policy Impact Research: Some Effects of Reliability on Validation," paper prepared for delivery at the Conference on the Measurement of Policy Impact, Tallahassee, Florida, May 6-8, 1971, p. 2.

CHAPTER VI: PART II

1. John G. Gunnell, "Deduction, Explanation, and Social Scientific Inquiry," *American Political Science Review*, 63, no. 4 (December, 1969), 1262.

2. *Ibid.*, p. 1246. Taking a similar position, Michael Scriven contends: "Explanations are context bound affairs. Completeness or correctness are notions without meaning except in a given context." "Truisms as the Ground for Historical Explanation," in Patrick Gardiner (ed.), *Theories of History* (Glencoe, Ill.: The Free Press, 1959), p. 450.

3. See Karl Mannheim, *Ideology and Utopia* (New York: Harcourt,

Brace and World, 1936); Robert Merton, *Social Theory and Social Structure* (Glencoe, Ill.: The Free Press, 1957).

4. Robert Brown, *Explanation in Social Science* (Chicago: Aldine, 1963), p. 41.

5. *Ibid.*, p. 50.

6. This is not to deny that particular commonsense explanations (as opposed to commonsense *definitions of explanation*) may possess scientific value (i.e., for heuristic purposes).

7. C. Wright Mills, *The Sociological Imagination* (London: Oxford University Press, 1959), p. 126.

8. George C. Homans, "Theory in Sociology," in Robert E. L. Faris (ed.), *Handbook of Modern Sociology* (Chicago: Rand McNally, 1964), pp. 951-976.

9. Contingency thus accrues from both the initial postulation of theoretical concepts in such a way that they are amenable to operationalization, and from the manner in which this operationalization is actually accomplished. For an analysis of the latter, see the discussion of "examplars" in Thomas S. Kuhn, *The Structure of Scientific Revolutions* (Chicago: University of Chicago Press, 1970), pp. 186-191. But this requirement does not imply that all the terms of a theory may be translated into empirical equivalents. To the contrary, terms in theory that are not explicitly defined in observational terms are necessary if the theory is to postulate hypothetical relations transcending a single class of phenomenon. Thus, contingency is an attribute of a theory as a whole, but not each of its component terms. See Ernst Nagel, *The Structure of Science* (New York: Harcourt, Brace and World, 1961), pp. 101-104; and Carl G. Hempel, *Aspects of Scientific Explanation* (New York: The Free Press, 1965), pp. 109-112, 182-222. Also relevant to the notion of contingency is Sartori's discussion of "conceptual stretching," and of the need for a taxonomy of concepts with definite and dichotomous empirical referants. Giovanni Sartori, "Concept Misformation in Comparative Politics," *American Political Science Review*, 64, no. 4 (December, 1970), 1033-1053.

10. Karl R. Popper, *The Poverty of Historicism* (London: Routledge and Kegan Paul, 1957), pp. 130-137.

11. A detailed elaboration of the relativist (or "historicist") position is provided in Eugene F. Miller, "Positivism, Historicism, and Political Inquiry," *American Political Science Review*, 66, no. 3 (September, 1972), 796-817.

12. Restrictive conventions are assumptions that have empirical implications (e.g., sustaining a theory where it would otherwise be falsified) but which are not themselves subject to falsification (because they are not included in the premises of a theory, and therefore are not logically related to its observational conclusion). The use of such devices must be judged in terms of the extent to which a theory *has* left itself open to refutation. According to Kaplan's formulation, every theory possesses a degree of analyticity, deriving from the extent to which it has been subjected to test. Explanation is to this extent "conventional" or "closed": defining reality by establishing restrictions upon it. Theory is, in contrast,

"empirical" or "open": to the extent reality *does* impinge on explanation and compel its modification. Abraham Kaplan, *The Conduct of Inquiry* (Scranton, Penna.: Chandler, 1964), pp. 100-103. Theory may be perceived as closed at the stage of its initial formulation, and open when being subjected to falsification. What is required is that every means of "closure" employed in theory construction be "opened" to falsification.

13. The definition of "adequacy" is to be understood in terms of a comparison with other available and relevant explanations.

14. See Eugene Meehan, *Explanation in Social Science: A System Paradigm* (Homewood, Ill.: The Dorsey Press, 1968), pp. 115-120.

15. Kaplan, *The Conduct of Inquiry*, pp. 311-322.

16. Popper, *The Poverty of Historicism*, pp. 130-137. See also Carl Hempel, *Aspects of Scientific Explanation* (New York: The Free Press, 1965). His thesis of deductive nomological explanation is an endorsement of unity of method for all empirical science, and reduces scientific explanation to a single and universal logical pattern.

17. See R. B. Angel, "Explanation and Prediction: A Plea for Reason," *Philosophy of Science*, 34, no. 3 (September, 1967), 276-282.

18. Norwood R. Hanson, "On the Symmetry Between Explanation and Prediction," *Philosophy Review*, 68 (1959), 349-358.

19. Popper, *The Poverty of Historicism*, pp. 133-134.

20. Thomas L. Thorson, *Biopolitics* (New York: Holt, Rinehart and Winston, 1970), pp. 56-71.

21. *Ibid.*, Preface.

22. Karl Popper, *Logik der Forchung* (1935). Interpreted in W. A. Sachting, "Deductive Explanations and Prediction," *Philosophy of Science*, 34, no. 1 (March, 1967), 41-52.

23. Thorson, *Geopolitics*. "Grand Theory" is Mills's concept: Mills, *The Sociological Imagination*, Chapter 2.

24. For an analysis of the various aspects of generalization, see Kaplan, *The Conduct of Inquiry*, Chapter 3.

25. Gunnell, "Deduction, Explanation, and Social Scientific Inquiry."

26. N. R. Hanson, *Patterns of Discovery* (Cambridge, Eng.: Cambridge University Press, 1958), p. 64; Kuhn, *The Structure of Scientific Revolutions*, especially Chapter 6; and also Kenneth F. Schaffner, "Correspondence Rules," *Philosophy of Science*, 36, no. 3 (September, 1969), 280-290.

27. Karl R. Popper, *The Logic of Scientific Discovery* (New York: Harper and Row, 1968), pp. 60-62.

28. For example, see the "Symposium on Scientific Explanation in Political Science," *American Political Science Review*, 63, no. 4 (December, 1969), 1233-1262; and May Brodbeck, "Explanation, Prediction, and Imperfect Knowledge," in her *Readings in the Philosophy of the Social Sciences* (New York: Macmillan, 1968), pp. 363-397. For an analysis of some of the "ideological" positions in this debate, see Michael W. Jackson, "The Application of Method in the Construction of Theory," *Canadian Journal of Political Science*.

29. This follows from the definition of reliable explanation, which requires that the premises of explanation be contingent upon and falsifiable by the events being explained, and hence that such events be deductible from the premises.

30. Norton E. Long, in Meehan, *Explanation in Social Science*, Foreword, p. vi.

31. Brodbeck, *Readings in the Philosophy of the Social Sciences*, p. 376.

32. *Ibid.*, p. 389. Brodbeck points out that from a syllogistic law, one can predict an individual event. From a statistical law (or any other kind of imperfect law), one can predict a mass event. Both predictions, she states, are deductive, though both are not syllogistic. See also Hempel, *Aspects of Scientific Explanation*, pp. 58-59, for a discussion of "certainty" as a relational concept that mediates between premises and conclusions, and not as a "modal qualifier" of either the premises or the conclusions themselves.

33. Popper, *The Poverty of Historicism*, p. 134.

34. See Note 26 above.

35. It should be noted that while established premises cannot furnish original conclusions, deduction from unestablished or new premises can do so.

36. Mills, *The Sociological Imagination*, Chapters 2 and 3.

37. Arthur S. Goldberg, "On the Need for Contextualist Criteria," *American Political Science Review*, 63, no. 4 (December, 1969), 1248-1249.

CHAPTER VII

1. Albert Somit and Joseph Tanenhaus, *American Political Science: A Profile of a Discipline* (New York: Prentice-Hall, 1964), p. 79. With the possible exception of attributes four and five, perceptions of career success are so repute-oriented as to have little or no connection with the epistemic quality of scholarship or knowledge.

Attribute	*Rank*
Volume of publication	1
School at which doctorate was taken	2
Having the right connections	3
Ability to get research support	4
Quality of publication	5
Textbook authorship	6
Luck or chance	7
School of first full-time appointment	8
Self-promotion ("brass")	9
Teaching ability	10

2. See John P. Robinson, Robert Athanasion, and Kendra B. Head, *Measures of Occupational Attitudes and Occupational Characteristics* (Ann

Arbor: University of Michigan, Institute for Social Research, Survey Research Center, 1969).

3. Repute is intimately related to status, which is fundamental to the operation of large organizations such as the modern academic profession. See Robert Presthus, *The Organizational Society* (New York: Alfred A. Knopf, Inc., 1965), pp. 94-97. For a documentation of repute concerns in a scientific profession see Anselm L. Strauss and Lee Rainwater, *The Professional Scientist: A Study of the American Chemist* (Chicago: Aldine Pub. Co., 1962).

4. This organizational tendency is described in Herbert A. Simon, Donald W. Smithburg, and Victor Thompson, *Public Administration* (New York: Alfred A. Knopf, Inc., 1959), chap. 18; Richard Cyert and James G. March, *A Behavioral Theory of the Firm* (Englewood Cliffs, N.J.: Prentice-Hall, Inc., 1963). The public affect for science in America is described in Spencer Klaw, *The New Brahmins* (New York: Wm. Morrow & Co., 1968).

5. The arbitrary and subjective side of repute in the "hard" sciences is described in James D. Watson, *The Double Helix* (New York: Antheneum, 1968).

6. See A. B. Bronwell, "The Coming Intellectual Revolution," paper presented at the Pan American Congress of Engineering, San Juan, Puerto Rico, Sept. 6-13, 1969. Bronwell describes what he terms the "Pied Piper effect of learned professional societies." Rocket pioneer Robert Goddard and architect Frank Lloyd Wright are cited as two notable examples of creative genius "snubbed off by the currently popular set that holds dominion in the universal and professional societies," which Bronwell describes as preferring to deal with rather narrowly defined and orthodox conceptions of reality.

7. As used in this analysis, the term "vocational" does not imply some Weberian frame of reference nor does it incorporate Sheldon Wolin's analysis, "Political Theory as a Vocation," *American Political Science Review*, 63, no. 4 (December, 1969), 1062-1082.

8. Descriptions of quasi-theory, falsification potentiality, and the requisites of scientific explanation appear in the previous chapter.

9. Prominent examples of vocational knowledge are: Gabriel Almond and G. Bingham Powell, *Comparative Politics: A Developmental Approach* (Boston: Little, Brown and Co., 1966); Karl W. Deutsch, *Nationalism and Social Communication: An Inquiry into the Foundations of Nationality* (Cambridge: M.I.T. Press, 1953); Gabriel Almond and Sidney Verba, *The Civic Culture* (Boston: Little, Brown and Co., 1965); Fred Riggs, *Administration in Developing Areas: The Theory of the Prismatic Society* (New York: Houghton Mifflin Co., 1964); Robert A. Dahl, *Who Governs?* (New Haven: Yale University Press, 1961); David Easton and Jack Dennis, *Children in the Political System: The Origins of Political Legitimacy* (New York: McGraw-Hill, 1969).

10. Major examples of such exhortations are: Gabriel Almond and James Coleman, *The Politics of Developing Areas* (Princeton: Princeton University Press, 1960), last chapter; Heinz Eulau, *The Behavioral Per-*

suasion (New York: Random House, 1963); David Easton, *The Political System* (New York: Alfred A. Knopf, 1953), chap. 2.

11. Easton, *loc. cit.*

12. A discussion of "scientific consciousness" appears in James N. Rosenau, "Moral Fervor, Systematic Analysis, and Scientific Consciousness in Foreign Policy Research," in Austin Ranney (ed.), *Political Science and Public Policy* (Chicago: Markham Publishing Co., 1968), pp. 197-236.

13. Easton, *op. cit.*, p. 40.

14. Substantive illustrations of over-claim appear in Chapter V in the section entitled "Logical Warrant."

15. Riggs, *op. cit.*; Anthony Downs, *An Economic Theory of Democracy* (New York: Harper, 1957); Victor A. Thompson, *Modern Organization: A General Theory* (New York: Alfred A. Knopf, Inc., 1964).

16. James C. Charlesworth (ed.), *Contemporary Political Analysis* (New York: The Free Press, 1967).

17. Such confusions are manifested in Almond and Powell, *op. cit.*, as illustrated in Chapter V in the section entitled "Logical Warrant."

18. Gabriel Almond, "Political Theory and Political Science," *American Political Science Review*, 60, no. 4 (December, 1966), 869-879; David B. Truman, "Disillusion and Regeneration: The Quest for a Discipline," *American Political Science Review*, 50, no. 4 (December, 1965), 865-873; Thomas Kuhn, *The Structure of Scientific Revolutions* (Chicago: University of Chicago Press, 1962).

19. Additional references to the relevance of Kuhn's classic are: David Easton, "The New Revolution in Political Science," *American Political Science Review*, 63, no. 4 (December 1969); Karl Deutsch, "On Political Theory and Political Action," *American Political Science Review*, 65, no. 1 (March, 1971); Heinz Eulau, "Changing Views of Representation," in Ithiel de Sola Pool (ed.), *Contemporary Political Science* (New York: McGraw-Hill, 1967).

20. Martin Landau, *Political Theory and Political Science* (New York: Macmillan Co., 1972), p. 64.

21. Margaret Masterman, "The Nature of a Paradigm," in Imre Lakatos and Alan Musgrave (eds.), *Criticism and the Growth of Knowledge* (Cambridge: Cambridge University Press, 1970), pp. 60-65.

22. Some of the most prominent of these are discussed by Landau. *op. cit.*, pp. 64-65.

23. See Stephen Toulmin, "Does the Distinction Between Normal and Revolutionary Science Hold Water?" in Lakatos and Musgrave, *op. cit.*, pp. 43-47; Karl R. Popper, "Normal Science and Its Dangers," in Lakatos and Musgrave, *op. cit.*, pp. 52-55.

24. Kuhn, *op. cit.*, pp. 17-18, and especially p. 10.

25. Wolin, *op. cit.*, p. 1063.   26. Almond, *op. cit.*, p. 875.

27. See the frustrations of 'applying" in any concrete way Rigg's "theory" of the prismatic society (Riggs, *op. cit.*) in James R. Brady, "Japanese Administration and the 'Sala' Model," in Nimrod Raphaelli

(ed.), *Readings in Comparative Administration* (Boston: Allyn and Bacon, Inc., 1967), pp. 433-450.
28. Wolin, *loc. cit.*
29. Almond, *op. cit.*, p. 875; Wolin, *op. cit.*, p. 1072.
30. Khun, *op. cit.*, chaps. 6 and 7. 31. *Ibid.*, pp. 49-52.
32. Almond, *op. cit.*, pp. 873-878.
33. Eugene J. Meehan, *Contemporary Political Thought: A Critical Study* (Homewood, Ill.: Dorsey Press, 1967), pp. 62-67.
34. Bruce E. Wright, "Normative Prescription and Political Theory," paper presented at the 1970 American Political Science Association meeting, Los Angeles, Sept. 8-12, 1970, p. 17.
35. Ithiel de Sola Pool, "Some Facts about Values," *PS*, III, no. 2 (Spring, 1970), 102-103.
36. The problems of professional ethics in this context are analyzed in Chapter IX.
37. This distinction is elaborated in Meehan, *op. cit.*, p. 62.
38. An epistemological critique of *The Civic Culture* appears in Chapter V, in the section entitled "Logical Warrant." Almond and Verba, *op. cit.*; Christian Bay, *The Structure of Freedom* (Stanford: Stanford University Press, 1958).
39. Intellectual currents bolstering this notion are described in Philip H. Melanson, "The Dominant Normative Paradigm and Political Science," *Political Science*, July, 1973, pp. 53-61.
40. Harold D. Lasswell, "The Policy Sciences of Development," *World Politics*, 17, no. 4 (January, 1965), 286-309, at 290.
41. Almond and Powell, *op. cit.*, pp. 327-328.

CHAPTER VIII

1. Ithiel de Sola Pool, "The Necessity for Social Scientists Doing Research for Governments," *Background*, 10 (1966), 111-112.
2. Robert E. Lane, "The Decline of Politics and Ideology in a Knowledgeable Society," *The American Sociological Review*, 31 (October, 1966), 649-662, at 657. Similar trends and phenomena are analyzed by Heinz Eulau, "Skill Revolution and Consultative Commonwealth," *American Political Science Review*, 61, no. 1 (March, 1973), 169-191.
3. The idealization of "applied knowledge" and its assumed beneficence are prominent features in Fritz Machlup, *The Production and Distribution of Knowledge in the United States* (Princeton: Princeton University Press, 1962).
4. Problems and dynamics of knowledge and policy are surveyed in Philip H. Melanson (ed.), *Knowledge, Politics, and Public Policy* (Cambridge, Mass.: Winthrop Publishers, Inc., 1973).
5. These two themes constitute the basic concerns of most of the public policy articles collected in Elisabeth T. Crawford and Albert D. Biderman (eds.), *Social Scientists and International Affairs* (New York: John Wiley

& Sons, Inc., 1969). Meaningful consideration of the nature and quality of knowledge in relation to public policy is absent in this broad range of articles.

6. Don K. Price, *Government and Science* (New York: New York University Press, 1954), p. 161.

7. *Ibid.*, p. 169. Price, for example, states: "In short, scientific discoveries . . . enlarge the opportunity and broaden the possibilities for discretionary judgment in governmental affairs, just as they do for the acquisition of further knowledge." However, the pursuit of reliable knowledge and explanatory theory does not assure that the scientist will produce knowledge that is perceived as useful or immediately necessary by policy makers. Note how the assumption of beneficent knowledge underlies Price's optimism about the utility of science. In reality, reliable knowledge may have the opposite result if heeded by policy makers. That is, it may serve to circumscribe options or discretionary judgments by demonstrating that certain assumed options are, in reality, either not possible or not prudent.

Views like Price's appear with specific reference to social sicence as well. An attempt to bridge the gap between policy and science through the assumption of beneficent knowledge provides the basic perspective of "The Policy Sciences," a volume prepared in 1951 by leading social scientists to argue a harmony of goals between social policy and social science.

8. A prime example of this orientation within political science itself is Heinz Eulau and James G. March (eds.), *Political Science*, Behavioral and Social Sciences Survey Series (Englewood Cliffs, N. J.: Prentice-Hall, 1969).

9. A general treatment of these concerns is found in Elisabeth T. Crawford, "The Informal Organization of Policy-Oriented Social Science," in Crawford and Biderman, *op. cit.*, pp. 69-84.

10. *Knowledge into Action: Improving the Nation's Use of the Social Sciences.* Report of the Special Commission on the Social Sciences of The National Science Board, published by the National Science Foundation, 1969, pp. 15-20.

11. See Lauriston R. King and Philip H. Melanson, "Knowledge and Politics: Some Experiences From the 1960s, *Public Policy*, 20, (Winter, 1972), 83-101.

12. See Yehezkel Dror, "Policy Analysts: A New Professional Role in Government Service," *Public Administration Review*, 27, no. 2 (September, 1967), 197-203.

To some extent, this drive for an increased and more technical policy role has been successful already; not necessarily with respect to the new role of "policy analyst," but in a number of other roles. Horowitz states: "Demand for operations research analysts, tactical data systems, war-gaming, and simulation experts now rivals the search for basic engineering personnel." I. L. Horowitz, *Professing Sociology* (Chicago: Aldine Pub. Co., 1968), p. 262.

13. D. S. Greenberg, "Research Priorities: New Program at NSF Re-

flects Shift in Values," *Science,* 1970, no. 3954 (October 9, 1970), 144-146, at 144.

14. This is a major thrust of the reports entitled "Behavioral and Social Sciences Survey Series." The volume specifically addressed to political science (March and Eulau, *op. cit.*) is weighted in this direction even more heavily than some of the others in the series. See Note 32, Chapter IX.

15. The formal and informal links in one policy area are described in Paul De Forest, "The Social Sciences in the Foreign Policy Subsystem of Congress," in Crawford and Biderman, *op. cit.,* pp. 135-150.

16. *Ibid,.* p. 145.

17. See a thoughtful exhortation for such knowledge by Harry Eckstein, "Political Science and Public Policy," in Ithiel de Sola Pool (ed.), *Contemporary Political Science* (New York: McGraw-Hill, 1967), p. 162.

18. This orientation may have been spawned by the "apolitical," "neutral" ideal of expertise and by the penchant of hard science (whose methods, goals, and development social scientists were increasingly trying to emulate) toward an "apolitical" view of itself. This is described in Joseph Haberer, *Politics and the Community of Science* (New York: Van Nostrand Reinhold, 1969), chaps. 5, 11, 12.

19. In part, this tradition stems from classic notions about the divergence of theory and practice, as found in Karl Mannheim, *Man and Society in an Age of Reconstruction* (New York: Harcourt Brace, 1940), pp. 164-173; and from analyses of role conflict, as in Robert K. Merton, *Social Theory and Social Structure* (Glencoe, Ill.: The Free Press, 1949), pp. 161-178, 384-386. A more recent manifestation of this traditional view is found in Harold D. Lasswell, *The Future of Political Science* (New York: Atherton Press, 1963).

20. For example, see Kenneth P. Langton, *Political Socialization* (New York: Oxford University Press, 1969), p. 179: "In conclusion, although the question of social control cannot escape its Orwellian connotations, the wise citizen and responsible public servant can enjoy unprecedented prerogatives for useful and humane intervention in the evolution of political systems." See also Eulau and March, *op. cit.,* p. 40. In the context of such questions as lowering the voting age, the authors advertise: "Political socialization studies offer the most comprehensive and reliable information we have on these questions and we may hope that policy makers will make increasing use of it."

21. Description of the many levels and contexts of the use of political science's expertise are provided by Horowitz, *op. cit.,* Part III; Thomas E. Cronin and Sanford D. Greenberg (eds.), *The Presidential Advisory System* (New York: Harper & Row, 1969).

Influence has many forms. Henry Kissinger's role as Presidential advisor and Secretary of State is one of the most impressive and direct. Beyond the highest elite levels of policy formation, political scientists (in concert with other social scientists) are also involved in the implementation of policy. See Edward W. Widner, *Technical Assistance in Public Administration Overseas* Chicago: (Public Administration Service, 1964).

Through their research and writing, political scientists can influence policy even though visible, formal access is lacking. Strategic thinkers such as Herman Kahn, Klaus Knorr, Thomas C. Shilling, Glenn Snyder, and Anatol Rapoport have had a tremendous impact upon the thinking of American military and defense organizations. See Joseph E. Swartz, "Strategic Thought: Methodology and Reality," in Charles A. McCoy and John Playford (eds.), *Apolitical Politics* (New York: Thomas Y. Crowell Co., 1967), pp. 55-74. Private operations such as Rand make a business of dealing in expertise, and political scientists play a prominent role. See Philip Green, "Science, Government, and the Case of RAND: A Singular Pluralism," *World Politics*, 20, no. 2 (January, 1968), 301-326. selected high-level army officers on such subjects as "Threats to America."

Another important source of influence is the teaching role. In broad terms, political science as an academic discipline communicates ideas and perspectives relevant to policy to thousands of students, some of whom will later become active participants in policy formation at the elite levels of government. More direct influence results form "teaching" existing elites. At the Hudson Institute, for example, Herman Kahn and his staff instruct selected high-level army officers on such subjects as "Threats to America."

The Hudson Institute, The Institute for Defense Analysis, Rand, and other corporations existing on government contracts for expertise have helped create a situation in which the army is largely dependent upon external sources for important kinds of expertise that it has not cultivated internally to the degree necessary for functional independence. See Ward Just, "Soldiers," *Atlantic*, October, 1970, pp. 59-98, especially p. 90.

22. Charles H. Backstrom, "The Social Scientist as Policy Maker or The Astigmatic Leading the Blind and Vice Versa," paper presented at 1961 American Political Science Association meeting, St. Louis, September 6-9. Reprinted in *The Use of Social Research in Federal Domestic Programs*, III, Committee on Government Operations (Washington, D. C.: Government Printing Office, 1967), p. 235.

23. Lane, *op. cit.*, pp. 657-658.   24. *Ibid.*, p. 660.

25. See H. H. Gerth and C. Wright Mills (eds.), *From Max Weber* (New York: Oxford University Press, 1958), pp. 196-244.

26. See, for example, Allen Schick, "Systems Politics and Systems Budgeting," *Public Administration Review*, 29, no. 2 (March-April, 1969), 137-151.

27. This is especially visible in highly developed totalitarian regimes, such as the USSR, where the priorities of totalitarian rule conflict with those of further technological advancement and administrative efficiency. See Karl W. Deutsch, "Cracks in the Monolith; Possibilities and Patterns of Disintegration in Totalitarian Systems," in Carl J. Friedrich (ed.), *Totalitarianism* (Cambridge, Mass.: Harvard University Press, 1954), pp. 308-333.

28. Lane's assessment parallels the "end of ideology" thesis. See Daniel Bell, "The End of Ideology in the West," in *The End of Ideology* (New York: The Free Press, 1960). In addition, it is consistent with the tendency to view "politics" as an irrational—if not unfortunate—

dimension of public policy. This tendency is described by Avery Leiserson, "The Politics of Science: Science Politics, Science Policy, Policy Science—The Whole Thing," *Polity*, 4, no. 1 (Fall, 1973), 123.

29. Harold L. Wilensky, *Organizational Intelligence: Knowledge and Policy in Government and Industry* (Basic Books, 1967), p. 191.

30. Eckstein, *op. cit.*, p. 160.

31. This legitimating potential of expertise is, in part, founded upon the respect for and deference to "knowledge" and "science" that pervades the knowledgeable society. This respect and deference is reflected in the prestige accorded the occupational roles of "college professor" and "scientist." In the North-Hatt occupational status ratings of 1963, "college professor" ranked fifth and "scientist" third within a field of ninety occupations. Several of the occupations ranking ahead of or close to college professor and scientist were actually more specified variations of one or both of these occupational roles:

Occupation	Rank
Government scientist	4 (tie)
Nuclear physicist	3 (tie)
Chemist	6 (tie)

Source: John P. Robinson, Robert Athanasion, Kendra B. Head, *Measures of Occupational Attitudes and Occupational Characteristics* (Ann Arbor, Mich.: Survey Research Center, 1969), pp. 360-361.

32. Aaron Wildavsky, "Practical Consequences of the Theoretical Study of Defense Policy," *Public Administration Review*, 25, no. 2 (March, 1965), 91-103. Wildavsky describes the use of external expertise as a style of decision making that is pervading not only the area of defense policy, but other policy areas as well (pp. 102-103). This style is especially prominent in the United States Army at the higher levels of policy and strategy. See Just, *op. cit.*, p. 90.

33. Lee Rainwater and William L. Yancey, *The Moynihan Report and the Politics of Controversy* (Cambridge: M.I.T. Press, 1967), p. 275.

34. The significance of this point does not rely upon a documentation of the number and intensity of previous instances of legitimation through the imitiation of reliably knowledgeable expertise. The mere potential of such instances, which is inherent because of the dominance of vocational knowledge, the dynamics of the consultant role, and the cultural predispositions of the knowledgeable society assures that this is an important consideration.

35. Wilbert E. Moore, *The Professions: Roles and Rules* (New York: Russell Sage Foundation, 1970), p. 88.

36. Jacob Murray Edleman, *The Symbolic Uses of Politics* (Urbana: University of Illinois Press, 1964).

37. Daniel P. Moynihan, *Maximum Feasible Misunderstanding* (New York: Free Press, 1969), p. 191.

38. Duncan McRae, Jr., "Social Science and the Sources of Policy: 1951-1970," *PS*, 3, no. 3 (Summer, 1970), 294-309, at 294.

39. See Bertrand de Jeuvenal, "On the Nature of Political Science," *American Political Science Review*, 55, no. 4 (December, 1961), 773-779.

40. This is the position elaborated by F. S. C. Northrop, *The Logic of the Sciences and Humanities* (New York: Macmillan Co., 1947).

41. See David Easton, "The Revolution in Political Science," *American Political Science Review*, 63, no. 4 (December, 1969), 1051-1061. Easton bemoans the lack of relevance in behavioralism and contends that post-behavioralism consciously strives for relevance (pp. 1051-1052). Marvin Surkin asserts that changing the constituency of knowledge production will change the profession's posture toward relevance: "Sense and Non-sense" *PS*, 2, No. 4 (Fall, 1969), 573-581.

42. Theodore J. Lowi, "The Politics of Higher Education: Political Science As a Case Study," in George J. Graham, Jr., and George W. Carey (eds.), *The Post-Behavioral Era: Perspectives on Political Science* (New York: David McKay Co., Inc., 1972), pp. 11-36, at p. 35.

43. *Ibid.*, p. 32. Author's emphasis.

CHAPTER IX

1. Wilbert E. Moore, *The Professions: Roles and Rules* (New York: Russell Sage Foundation, 1970), p. 18.

2. *Ibid.*, p. 117.

3. This is a prominent theme in some of the critiques associated with the Caucus for a New Political Science. See Alan Wolfe, "Unthinking about the Thinkable: Reflections on the Failure of the Caucus for a New Political Science," *Politics and Society* 1, no. 3 (May, 1971), 393-406; Marvin Surkin and Alan Wolfe (eds.), *An End to Political Science* (New York: Basic Books, 1970).

4. A survey of ethical problems in social science appears in Gideon Sjoberg (ed.), *Ethics, Politics, and Social Research* (Cambridge, Mass.: Schenkman Publishing Co., Inc. 1967). See also Irving Lewis Horowitz, *Professing Sociology* (Chicago: Aldine Publishing Co., 1968), pp. 295-304.

5. Descriptions of professional "processes" appear in Albert Somit and Joseph Tanenhaus, *American Political Science: A Profile of a Discipline* (New York: Atherton Press, 1964); Philip H. Melanson, "The Political Science Profession, Political Knowledge, and Public Policy," *Politics and Society*, vol. 2, no. 4 (Summer, 1972), pp. 489-501.

6. Sjoberg, *op. cit.*, pp. 141-61.

7. Jerome Stephens, "Political, Social, and Scientific Aspects of Medical Research on Humans," *Politics and Society*, 3, no. 4 (Summer, 1973), 409-435, at 413. Quotation from Walter Modell, "Comment on Some Fallacies and Errors."

8. Final Report of the American Political Science Association Committee on Professional Standards and Responsibilities, "Ethical Problems of Academic Political Scientists" (Washington, D.C.: American Political Science Association, 1968), pp. 11-13. The AAUP statement is reprinted in PS, II, no. 4 (Fall, 1969), 654-655.

9. *American Political Science Review*, LXIV, no. 2 (June, 1970), 589.

10. PS, VI, no. 4 (Fall, 1973), 434, "Annual Business Meeting."

11. Leonard D. Cane, Jr., "The AMA and the Gerontologists: Uses and Abuses of 'A Profile of the Aging,' " in Sjoberg, op. cit., pp. 78-114.

12. Report from the Center for the Study of Democratic Institutions, Anti-Ballistic Missile System: Yes or No? (New York: Hill and Wang, 1969), p. xxiv.

13. Joseph Haberer, Politics and the Community of Science (New York: Van Nostrand Reinhold Co., 1969), pp. 310-322.

14. Operations Research Society of America (ORSA) "Report on Professional Standards," 1969.

15. George W. Rathjens, Steven Weinberg, Jerome B. Weisner, "Comments on the Ad Hoc ORSA Committee Report on Professional Standards," September 29, 1971.

16. William Buchanan, "The Market for Doctoral Instruction in Political Science," paper presented at the 1967 annual meeting, American Political Science Association, Chicago; "Profile of Ph.D. Recipients in Political Science, in 1968," PS, II, no. 4 (Fall, 1969), 659.

17. See Knowledge into Action: Improving the Nation's Use of the Social Sciences, Report of the Special Commission on the Social Sciences of the National Science Board (Washington, D.C.: U. S. Government Printing Office, 1964). The exhortation for "better," more rigorous data pervades the various recommendations and analyses concerning improved "use" of social science expertise.

18. Haberer, op. cit., p. 322.

19. Thomas S. Kuhn, The Structure of Scientific Revolutions (Chicago: University of Chicago Press, Phoenix Edition, 1964). Ambiguities in Kuhn's concept of paradigm are discussed in Israel Scheffler, Science and Subjectivity (New York: Bobbs-Merrill, 1967). A survey and analysis of the political science literature relating to the application of Kuhn's thesis to the discipline is found in Martin Landau, Political Theory and Political Science (New York: The Macmillan Co., 1972), ch. 2.

20. Heinz Eulau, The Behavioral Persuasion (New York: Random House, 1963), p. 137.

21. Ithiel de Sola Pool, "Some Facts about Values," PS, 3, no. 4 (Spring, 1970), 105.

22. Meehan, op cit., p. 56.

23. David Braybrooke and Alexander Rosenberg, "Comment: Getting the War News Straight," American Political Science Review, LXVI, no. 3 (September, 1972), 818-826, at 826.

24. See John G. Gunnell, "The Idea of Conceptual Framework: A Philosophical Critique," Journal of Comparative Administration, 1, no. 1, 140-176; "Symposium on Scientific Explanation in Political Science," American Political Science Review, LXIII, no. 4 (December, 1969), 1233-1262; "Positivism, Historicism, and Political Inquiry," American Political Science Review, LXVI, no. 3 (September, 1972), 796-873. These discussions examine debates in philosophy of science and their relevance to political science.

25. Gabriel Almond, "Political Theory and Political Science," American

Political Science Review, 60, no. 4 (December, 1966), 869-879; David B. Truman, "Disillusion and Regeneration: The Quest for a Discipline," *American Political Science Review,* 59, no. 4 (December, 1965), 865-873.

26. David C. Leege, "On Measurement of Dependent Variables in Policy Impact Research: Some Effects of Reliability on Validation," paper presented at the Conference on the Measurement of Policy Impact, Tallahassee, Florida, May 6-8, 1971, p. 2.

27. See Sjoberg, *op, cit.*

28. From a different perspective, William E. Connolly has argued that a "responsible ideology" in political science would not demand of opposing ideas a rigor and scientism it cannot itself produce. Connolly's idea recognizes the unfair advantages that the profession often bestows upon the value positions codified in vocational knowledge. His imperative is aimed more at value discourse than at the uses and abuses of political knowledge. Because the latter are the crux of the profession's ethical responsibility to itself as a discipline and to the political systems in which it exists, the conception of responsibility offered here is more epistemologically oriented than Connolly's. William E. Connolly, *Political Science and Ideology* (New York: Atherton Press, 1967), pp. 146-147. The notion of responsibility and its relevance to epistemology, as well as many of the substantive illustrations in this chapter, appear in the author's "On The Interaction of Epistemic Canons and Professional Ethics In Political Science," *Political Methodology,* forthcoming.

29. Heinz Eulau, "Political Science," in Bert Hoselitz (ed.), *A Reader's Guide to the Social Sciences* (Glencoe, Ill.: The Free Press, 1960), p. 89. Eulau asserts that "political science has been freed from the quest for certainty." He fails to distinguish "certainty" from epistemological validity. Moreover, freedom from the quest for certainty cannot mean freedom from a sense of responsibility toward inquiry. Very often those who dismiss certainty dismiss considerations of validity as well. See Yehezkel Dror, "The Barriers Facing Policy Science," *American Behavioral Scientist,* 7 no. 5 (January, 1964), 4.

30. One confusion leading to irresponsible claims concerns attributing to a model, classificatory schema, or descriptive framework the explanatory capacities and rigor of a theory. Gabriel Almond and Sidney Verba, *The Civic Culture* (Boston: Little Brown, 1965), and Gabriel Almond and G. Bingham Powell, *Comparative Politics: A Developmental Approach* (Boston: Little Brown, 1966), are two prominent examples of works that implicitly and explicitly claim theoretical and explanatory capacities but lack the refinement of operational indicators, the precision of hypothesization, and the rigorous integration and empirical vulnerability needed for explanatory, theory. See Chapter V, pp. 112-118.

31. The idea of "logical warrant" is elaborated by Norton E. Long, Forward, p. vi, of Eugene J. Meehan, *Explanation in Social Science: A System Paradigm* (Homewood, Ill.: The Dorsey Press, 1968). See Chapter V, pp. 112-15. One example of the propensity to exceed logical warrant is manifested in a study of Jamaican school children from various class

backgrounds that focused upon the socializing influence of the peer group in the school environment. The author does not hesitate to leap to a systemic level of speculation about the manipulative potentials of his findings. "If, for example, social planners in the Caribbean felt the task of industrialization required two immediate political goals, namely (1) to maintain a climate of political support for the regime and (2) to dis-courage—by non-coercive means—excessive political participation, they would do well to segregate working class students from those of higher classes because, as public education is expanded, and working class stu-dents are allowed to mingle with their higher status peers, they become more politicized and less supportive of the political regime."

Disregarding the tremendous normative implications of such counsel, the "data" in which it is purportedly grounded are far too limited in focus and epistemology to warrant valid speculation concerning develop-mental possibilities at the regime level. Kenneth P. Langton, *Political Socialization* (New York: Oxford University Press, 1969), p. 178.

32. Heinz Eulau and James G. March (eds.), *Political Science* (Engle-wood Cliffs, N.J.: Prentice-Hall, 1969). Neil J. Smeiser and James A. Davis (eds.), *Sociology* (Englewood Cliffs, N. J.), provide an interesting contrast in the responsibility of broad assessments. These works are part of a series called "Behavioral and Social Sciences Survey." *Sociology* describes that discipline's public policy role in terms of the conflicts, ten-sions, and ethical problems surrounding the uses and abuses of knowl-edge. *Political Science* discusses the public policy role almost exclusively through advertisements of willingness and ability to "serve." Not only is a cognizance of the ethical dilemmas posed in *Sociology* absent in *Political Science,* but the only "obligation" depicted is that the political scientist conduct his research in a manner tailored to the needs of policy makers. The epistemological capacity of knowledge is not considered. The orienta-tion of *Political Science* suggests the adoption of a "let the buyer beware" posture. In place of reasoned analysis about ethical issues relating to re-search, one finds an almost pathological fixation with "service." More importantly, the urge to "serve" results in an inflated description of epistemic capacity and a neglect of the epistemic limitations of contempo-rary political science (pp. 51-55).

33. The criteria cited take their inspiration from Karl Mannheim, *Ideology and Utopia: An Introduction to the Sociology of Knowledge,* trans. Louis Worth and Edward Shils (New York: Harvest Books, 1936); and Robert K. Merton, *Social Theory and Social Structure* (Glencoe, Ill.: The Free Press, 1968 edition), pp. 460-488.

34. The perspective and much of the substance contained in these sug-gestions are taken from Edgar Litt and Philip H. Melanson, "A Peer Group of Liberals: The Profession and Its Public Discontents," a paper delivered at the 1969 annual meeting of the American Political Science Association, New York, September 1-5.

INDEX

About the Author

Philip H. Melanson is an associate professor of Political Science at Southeastern Massachusetts University. He received a Ph.D. in political science from the University of Connecticut in 1972. He has been a contributor to *Polity, American Political Science Review, Politics and Society, Public Policy, Society,* and other scholarly journals. He is the editor of *Knowledge, Politics, and Public Policy* (Winthrop, 1973).